A *heart* FILLED WITH *love* HAS NO
CHOICE BUT TO *heal*

Every Mum
has
Magic
Kisses

To Rose
Love Ber

Ber Collins

www.bercollins.ie

Ordering Information
Quantity sales. Special discounts are available on quantity purchases by institutions, schools, associations, charities and others. For details, contact the publisher at the address above.

Printed in the Republic Of Ireland

ISBN 978-1-5262-0001-3

Disclaimer: This book is not intended as a substitute for the medical advice of physicians. The reader should regularly consult a physician in matters relating to his/her health and particularly with respect to any symptoms that may require diagnosis or medical attention.

To
"Team Collins"
I love us xx

ACKNOWLEDGEMENTS

Thank you to my family who, despite the difficult subject, have supported me in the writing of this book. I want to thank my Mum especially with whom I have laughed and cried. We are on an amazing journey of healing together.

To my Dad – for my journey.

Thank you to Tracy Aspel of "The Creative Institute"; our chance meeting was the beginning of this book coming to life. The hours we spent talking and recording, together with her gentle probing questions, helped produce a structure for the book. Her encouragement and feedback along the way were just what I needed to persevere with my writing.

I entrusted my completed book to a few people to read in its early stages and their gentle feedback was insightful and very much appreciated. Thank you Marianne Dwyer and Theresa Rock.

To Neil McCarthy who helped with editing, guiding me towards greater clarity – I knew within five minutes of speaking with him that he 'got me' and my message. He has been a joy to work with, ever gentle and sensitive to the nature of the book, and yet cool and objective.

This book would not be in your hands without the help of Ruán Dignam of RD Marketing and Media who has guided me smoothly through the whole process.

Thank you to Elaine Hennessy of Little Blue Studio for bringing my dream for the cover of the book to life.

And finally to John, David and Laura; thank you for your endless support and love. I love you guys.

CONTENTS

INTRODUCTION

"HEALING DOESN'T MEAN THE DAMAGE NEVER EXISTED, IT MEANS THE DAMAGE NO LONGER CONTROLS OUR LIVES" - AKSHAY DUBEY

I see so many people in my clinic suffering from the effects of an unhappy childhood: people suffering from depression and anxiety, filled with anger and sadness at a childhood lost to abuse of various forms, people who are afraid or unable to love, full of blame for the people who hurt them. Their hearts are broken and empty, and they can see no way out of the cycle of sadness, anger and fear. Mothers, in particular, finding it difficult to be the kind of mum they would like to be because, perhaps, they have not been shown love themselves as a child and they are so consumed with their own pain that there is no space for anyone else.

This is a story of hope for all the women and men out there who feel they did not receive the love and care they needed, as children, to help them grow into the confident and loving adults their own children need. I discovered that it is possible for someone who has had a less than idyllic childhood to be a great parent and be happy again. Each one of us has the power to heal our pain and become the kind of mum or dad we want to be. However we need to have a desire for something different in order for healing to occur. Desire is what motivates us to do everything.

"Every Mum Has Magic Kisses" is the story of a girl who was sexually abused by her father and kept it a secret. She was afraid to tell anyone because he told her he would die if she did.

This is her story, my story.

Last year I met a young woman who had stage four cancer. She was married to a man she loved and together they had a daughter. She was diagnosed with a very aggressive form of cancer while she was pregnant with this little girl. Her fear around maybe having to leave her family in the future was preventing her from allowing herself to truly feel the love she had in her heart for her daughter. We worked together over the next few months and she found herself letting go of the fear and embracing all the love she had for her child. One day she sat opposite me and said: "Ber, you and I are the same; you have today and I have today", and this is how she lived those final months of her life: filled with love and happiness. We went on a journey together, discovering and really understanding the difference between healing and curing. Even though she didn't get the cure she wanted she filled her final months with love for her husband, her little girl and her family. She taught me so much and encouraged me to write this book as she said she would love to have it if she were around to raise her daughter.

The name for the book came to me one day while I was out walking. I was really struggling with writing the book as it's not something I have ever done before. I couldn't understand this desire that kept gnawing away at me but it just wouldn't go away. I knew it was something I had to do; it was the next piece of the puzzle that is my life: to share what I have learned with you so that you can find the happiness that is waiting for you. Fortunately I live in the countryside so no one was there to see me walking along muttering to myself, arguing with myself about whether I would or would not write this book. I really did feel as if something or someone was guiding me and pushing me and so, in frustration one day, as I was walking the dog I asked out loud: "Ok if I'm really meant to write this book, then whoever or whatever is guiding me to do this really needs to help me out here because I am struggling – big time". Immediately the name of the book popped into my head. It felt like such a perfect name for it that I decided to forge ahead and see if I could write it.

When my kids fell and hurt themselves they ran to me to make it better. "Kiss it better Mum", they said, and I did. When they needed someone to dry their tears they knew that a hug and a kiss from me or their Dad would make everything better. They climbed up on our laps to get the comfort they needed. When they felt sad they believed I had the power to make them feel better. According to them I had magic kisses. No matter how bad they were feeling or how sore a knee was, a kiss from Mum or Dad fixed everything. They didn't know or care what I had been through in my childhood; they didn't see me as broken or damaged, and it didn't make me less of a mum in their eyes. They simply believed that I could perform magic. I found that I could and so can you.

My wish for you is that by the time you get to the end of this book you will have reached down inside yourself and found the strength you need. It's there for you now to help you on this journey to be happy and free of your past. You can do it. If you really want to turn your life around, just trust that this is exactly where you are meant to be in this moment. Your children need your loving arms, your kisses, your smiles so that they can be happy too. You are there to show them. Teach them. It's a very important job and you can do it. You are their mum, their teacher, their friend and it's your job to guide them, love them and help them on their journey to adulthood.

How you treat them will be how they will learn to treat themselves. The words you speak to them will be the words they use inside their heads to talk to themselves.

You can show them that they deserve to be loved and accepted for who they are just as you deserved to be when you were small. It's time to step up, take what you need from your past, put it in a knapsack on your back, and walk away from the stuff that brings you down. You can walk on boldly, trusting that each step will bring you further away from the pain and into a place where you can feel happiness again. You have what it takes. We all do.

CHAPTER 1

MY STORY

I was eight years old when I was sexually abused by my Dad. I remember the first time it happened like it was yesterday. I stood on the landing afterwards in my lilac nightdress which was a little too long and which used get caught under my feet. The picture of a princess on the front seemed to mock me. I couldn't believe what had just happened. I didn't understand it. It felt so wrong and yet he had told me it was ok - this is what all little girls did. I didn't like it. And then a week later it happened again and then again and again. I became afraid every time he came near me. When he was home I tried to make myself really small in the hope he might not notice me. I was afraid to be left alone with him. My world changed. I can't remember what it was like before. I remember years of being afraid to go to sleep until he was in bed. I was always on guard, waiting. My thoughts every day were consumed with "Will it happen today?", "Where is he?", "No Mum please don't go to town and leave me alone with him". I began to wet the bed. Night after night I woke feeling ashamed at the mess I had made. I began to have bad dreams. I had the same nightmare over and over again where I was being chased by a man with a gun up the road where I lived. I knew that if he caught me he would kill me. In my dream, I ran into the back of a neighbour's house where I jumped into a dustbin. I pulled the lid down over my head and tried not to breathe, trying to make myself invisible. I heard his footsteps come closer and closer until suddenly the lid of the dustbin was lifted and a gun was put to my head. I woke suddenly, crying out, each time the sound of the gunshot ringing in my ears. My parents were frustrated with me. No-one made the connection. Inside my head I was screaming but nobody heard. I couldn't tell anybody what was happening but I hoped someone would find out and make it stop. I pleaded with my eyes but nobody noticed.

Because of my behaviour I got extra attention and I needed that. I was a cheeky little thing who loved to be noticed. I loved to sing and act goofy. I loved trying to make people laugh with my antics. In a family with four children I suddenly became the special one to him and it felt good yet bad. When my younger sister had arrived when I was five and a half she had taken my place as the baby of the family. No one seemed to think I was cute any more. I was told to grow up, that I was the big girl and I had to start acting like it now and it hurt. The new baby was really cute, especially in those soft orange pyjamas she wore, and I loved her but I still wanted her to go back to wherever she had come from and let me be the baby again. But she didn't, she was here to stay and everyone loved her. When the abuse began I felt special again, I was Daddy's special little girl again and we had a secret. That was nice – sort of. It was so confusing.

When I started secondary school at twelve years of age, I used pass a church every day on my way home from school. Day after day I stood on the steps trying to get the courage to go inside and ask a priest if what my Dad was telling me was true – that this was what all little girls did. I was so afraid of going in and asking. Week after week went by and I just could not find the courage to go in. Finally one Monday afternoon, after a particularly horrible and upsetting weekend, I ran in the door and straight into the confessional. The little hatch opened and the priest said his few words. I quickly spluttered out my question. The priest's response was to ask me if I knew what a climax was and, when I said no, he told me I didn't know what I was talking about and that I was being silly. I ran out the door; that was the first and last time I spoke about it until many years later.

The abuse continued until I was fourteen when one day, as his hands slipped under the covers when he came to sprinkle holy water on my forehead and kiss me goodnight, I hissed at him to 'fuck off'. He was shocked and he did.

The abuse stopped but, from then on, whenever he came near me, even to just place his hand on my shoulder in an affectionate way, I would shrink away, the memories vivid and clear in my head. Life went on and neither of us ever mentioned what had happened.

I must have presented a very vulnerable face to the outside world because, at the same time as I was being abused at home, I was being bullied at school. When I was about ten years old a group of girls from a class above me began bullying me every day after school. They stood leaning against a wall waiting until I came out and then pushed and pulled at my coat and schoolbag. The whole time they were calling me names. Some of the names were worse than the ones I called myself. Some days I delayed as long as I could in the classroom putting my books in my bag, hoping they would be gone by the time I came out. But they were always there, laughing and jeering, a gang of four against one. I always kept my head down and kept walking, their words of how useless and stupid I was echoing in my ears. Occasionally I shouted something back at them, but I usually kept walking as fast as I could, trying to get to the turn in the road when they would go a different way to me. One day things got totally out of control when three of them held me against a wall and the other one beat and kicked me. She hit me across the head with my own schoolbag, thumped me in the stomach, and kicked me for several minutes in both my shins. This happened on a main road with traffic passing up and down and no one stopped to help. That evening I ended up in a doctor's surgery when both my legs went completely black from the beating. At this point my parents stepped in and approached the school. The bullies were threatened with expulsion and never came near me again.

At seventeen and just three months away from taking my Leaving Certificate Examinations, a teacher at school insisted I could no longer be part of the class for, of all things, smiling. I was told I could not come back into class for the remainder of the year and that I was to study the rest of the syllabus on my own. When I got home and told my parents, my father went to the Head Nun to plead my case and get me reinstated in the class. Nobody approached me for the next few days and then one lunch time, when everyone was leaving the school building to enjoy some fine weather, I was called to the Head Nun's office. She sat on a chair on the far side of her desk and asked me to sit on a high stool at the other side. I felt awkward and vulnerable perched on a high stool with the nun leaning back in her chair looking up at me. Her first words were: "You must be a terrible disappointment to your parents. Your sister, so bright and intelligent, and then they have you. You're stupid and you will never amount to anything". This was totally unexpected. I thought I was going to be told to have more respect for the teacher or to pay more attention in class. The nun went on and on telling me how bad, stupid, and useless I was until I couldn't keep it in any longer. The tears finally flowed. I had tried to stay strong but the words hurt. Her words, I remember, resonated at a very deep level with me. I always kept the cheery face on for the world, but inside, these were the words I used with myself. Once I was crying the nun sat back and smiled. She reached into the drawer of the desk, took out a packet of tissues, and handed them to me. I was now crying like a baby with red eyes and running nose. As she handed me the tissue, she smiled sweetly and said: "I bought these for you at lunchtime – I knew you would need them. Now go back to class".

With very heavy steps, red eyes, and an aching heart, I went back to class. I felt so terribly small, sad, and broken into tiny little pieces.

During the abuse I was confused and torn between love, hate, and fear for this man I loved and trusted, who had abused my trust in the most unimaginable way. I felt abused at school too, my feelings disregarded and thrown aside as if I was nothing and did not matter. I felt sad and isolated. I felt used. I felt like a nuisance in the family. I became cheeky and bold until I was told one day that it was becoming increasingly difficult to love me. That stung. That hurt. I was filled with resentment. "If you only knew", I used say in my head. "I'm the one keeping this family together – If I told my story this family would be ripped apart". The resentment grew and grew. I thought of how, if I wanted to, I could blackmail him. I was very angry. And then, when I was 21, my Dad died. In the moments before he died he turned to me and said: "I love you". And I cried. I still loved him and had wanted to be able to talk to him about what he had done and make things ok between us. My chance was gone.

Chapter 2

If you don't have a dream
how you are going to have a dream come true?

As a child I loved to watch *Little House on the Prairie*, *The Brady Bunch* and *The Waltons*. I could be found glued to the television every time one of these programmes came on. For thirty minutes I could escape to a world where kids were happy and safe. I imagined I lived with them. I wanted to be Laura Ingles. The kids were happy, loved, and they were tucked up in bed at night free from fear.

I escaped into books. Enid Blyton was a life saver. I read everything she wrote. The *Famous Five*, *Secret Seven* and *Malory Towers* were all books I lost myself in when I was young. In my head I was part of the gang, happy and carefree, having adventures, drinking ginger beer, and putting the bad guys in jail.

I loved fairy tales like *Snow White* and *Cinderella*, and from a very young age I dreamt of having my own family. I dreamed about the kind of man I would marry, and used go to an imaginary place in my head where I had a family of my own. There I had two children, a boy and a girl, who I hugged and kissed, talked to, played silly games with, and who I tucked up in bed with a story - all the things I wanted for myself. I played out the programmes I loved with my dolls, and I was at my happiest when I was playing 'house' and tucking those make-believe children up in little shoe boxes, the small blankets secured up under their chins.

Those dreams stayed with me as I grew up and kept me going through difficult times. I didn't know how, but I just knew those dreams would come true.

After the incident with the nun I was very angry for a long time. Every so often I went through, in my head, all the things I could have said in retort if I had been brave enough. I played the scene over and over again, each time feeling more sad and angry than before. And then the memories with Dad would surface again and I felt even worse. One day I realised that, even though I had finished school, and was now working, this nun was still making me feel sad and angry and that realisation made me even angrier. I was cross at myself for letting her make me feel that way and so I made a decision. I decided there and then that the nun would no longer have this effect on me. I decided that it was over – no matter how many times I played the scene over in my head it would always end the same way so I decided to stop. The best way to show that nun was to go away and make something of myself, be happy, successful and strong. I decided to do the same regarding the experiences with Dad. I knew that feeling sorry for myself, being sad, angry, or bitter would only serve to hurt myself. My Dad was dead and he couldn't hurt me again.

I didn't realise it at the time but this was when I built a wall around me to protect myself from any more pain. It was thick and strong and I was safe behind it.

I first met John when we were both 13 years old. Well we didn't meet as such. Myself and a pal from school used attend a music theory class and we both fancied him. We used watch, mesmerised, when the teacher would ask us for help to move the piano out of the way so that she could teach the class, and John would use his athletic frame to easily and effortlessly oblige. He made what used be a boring theory class into something I looked forward to. Each week we waited to see if he would arrive and we spent a lot of the class whispering and trying not to stare at him as young girls tend to do. The following year he attended a different class than I did, so I didn't meet him again for a few years. When I was sixteen I joined a folk group in our local church and this became a great outlet for me. It was a mix of boys and girls who were all interested in music and singing. As I made lots of new friends my confidence grew. My role was as one of the violinists for the group, and we met regularly for practice and social outings. Weekends away with the group were filled with fun, groups of us often sitting around a fire with mugs of coffee while one of the guys played the guitar and the rest of us sang. They were innocent days filled with fun and laughter and I loved them. No-one needed to know any more about me than I wanted to tell and I was accepted for exactly who I was.

I loved those days even more when a new guy asked to join the group. He was going to join as a guitarist and we were all curious to see who it was and what he would be like. Imagine my surprise when the guy who walked in was John from my theory class. Over the next year we gradually became really good friends, socialising together and spending long hours chatting, solving the problems of the world, often into the early hours of the morning. We just seemed to click. We began to go out as a foursome with my brother and his girlfriend, but it wasn't until the night of our Leaving Cert results that we acknowledged the spark between us. We were celebrating with friends at a nightclub, and having great fun dancing together, when the tempo changed to a slow set. Those slow sets were a great opportunity for a snog. Up until this John and I would always have sat down as soon as a slow set came on but this night was different. The song was *Tonight I Celebrate My Love*" by Peabo Bryson and Roberta Flack and it was the most natural thing in the world for us to kiss. I went home on cloud nine that night, the 12th of August 1983, with the memory of that kiss lingering on in my mind. John and I became inseparable and, even though we were very young, John asked me to marry him when we were nineteen. We both wanted similar things, one of the most important being to create a family filled with love and happiness and so, of course, I said yes. We kept our plans a secret for two years as we were sure people would try to talk us out of it because we were so young. When we were both twenty-one we decided to get engaged and share our plan with our families.

We had already started saving for a house, meeting every Friday with our wages, and lodging a big chunk of it into a joint savings account. We had very little money left over and John was going to sell his record player and speakers to buy me a ring. Being asked to join a band for weddings spared him parting with his much loved musical equipment. We went shopping, finally settling on a simple diamond and sapphire ring. Our families were delighted for us, and two years later, five years to the day after our first kiss, we were married. My father was dead by then and so my brother walked me up the aisle. We didn't need any sheets of paper with our vows written down as we looked into each other's eyes and promised to love each other for the rest of our lives. The sun shone on us and we had an amazing day surrounded by friends and family. And so our married life began.

The happiness I felt as I embarked on this new journey helped me to block out the pain of my childhood as I concentrated on this new life my husband and I wanted to create. I never forgot what had happened, but I believed I was strong enough to move on, and that my childhood dreams of having a family were enough to help me put it all behind me. I was in love and that was all that mattered. I felt safe and happy with a man who loved me deeply and knew how to show it. We were busy working, paying a mortgage, having fun and settling into married life. Then when we were twenty-five our son was born. This was the start of my childhood dreams coming true. A family of my own, a husband who I loved and who loved me, and now a child of my own.

Chapter 3

Our children arrive

In March, 1990, the pregnancy test confirmed it. I was pregnant. Apart from my wedding day this was the happiest I had been in my whole life. My dreams were coming true. I was going to be a Mum. Every night I dreamt about what it would be like. I imagined what the baby would look like asleep and how I would look in at him until he sleepily opened his eyes and then looked for a feed. We were determined that this little baby would fit into our lives and nothing much would change. We were in for a shock.

It was the 5th December, 1990, and I was sitting up in my hospital bed eating tea and toast when the gynaecologist arrived into the room and said: "There's a bed free in the labour ward. Follow me". Now I don't know about you but those words were enough to make me choke on my toast and splutter my tea all over the crisp white sheets. "But but, my husband isn't here, I'm not ready, no one said I'm going to have it now". My heart was beating so loud and fast in my chest that I thought I was going to die. Without a minute to gather myself I was whisked away (well more like manoeuvred) up to the labour ward where my labour was induced. My husband arrived, and three hours and fifty minutes later, I was holding this six pounds three ounces , chicken legged, squawking little bundle in my arms. My husband kept commenting on how big his little feet were and the pride and delight on his face made everything ok.

I don't remember much of the rest of that day but I do remember having a sense of: "That's it now – there's no going back". The nurses came and went keeping an eye on David for the first hour or two, and then told me that I could start looking after him myself. (We agreed fairly quickly on a name for him – we both liked the idea of a strong solid name and

'David' in a funny way seemed to suit this little fella). Left alone with this baby I realised I hadn't a clue. I had never changed a nappy or fed a baby before. I was only five when my younger sister was born and none of my siblings had kids at this stage. During the pregnancy I fully intended breastfeeding as I had read all about it in my books that I devoured throughout the nine months, and I was determined to do absolutely everything right. This was part of my dream. I had the rocking chair at home with big fluffy cushions where I had imagined myself and my baby would sit bonding as I breastfed. I was going to give this baby the perfect start. My body however had other ideas. The nurse came in to start helping me with my breastfeeding, took one look at me and said: "This is not going to work – your nipples are too flat, you should have been working on them throughout the pregnancy". "Huh? Working on them?" was all I could say as I let her take David away to give him a bottle. I remember thinking to myself: "What kind of mum am I that I can't even breastfeed my baby?" But then I was so exhausted at that stage, all I really wanted to do was sleep. I was still sleepy with the gas they had given me because I had sucked on that tube for all I was worth. And I was also feeling drunk from the pethidine they had injected me with. A short while later the nurse arrived back with David, telling me that he wouldn't take the bottle and that she would try him again in a while as "He's probably tired – the little mite". "He's tired?" I said to myself, not really feeling sympathetic, I must admit. So the nurse left the room and I sat there on the bed looking at this little guy who was now starting to whinge. I rocked the little cot gently but the whinges got louder and louder until they were a full blown cry. A nurse put her head around the door saying: "Check his nappy". "Check it yourself", I felt like saying. Do you realise I am totally and utterly exhausted? So there I was hovering over the cot, not even knowing how to hold this little creature, undoing the baby grow, feeling completely at a loss as to what I was going to do when I did get the nappy undone. I kept going, undid the nappy and what I saw (which no one had prepared me for) was a big mess of black stuff.

14

What do I do? Not having a clue what it was or how to deal with it, I sat on the side of the bed and cried. This isn't how it's supposed to be I thought to myself. This wasn't how I had imagined things. I cried and cried and the baby cried and cried and it was that scene that my friend who worked in the hospital came across when she came up to bring me a cup of tea. She took one look at the pair of us, me sobbing on the bed, David screaming in the cot with his little legs kicking the air in frustration, and in 60 seconds the baby was changed and tucked up snug as a bug in his cot, and I was tucked into bed with my pillows fluffed and a steaming cup of tea in my hand. Superwoman wouldn't have got a look-in, it was like Mother Teresa had entered my room and just made everything ok – for that moment anyway. My friend reassured me that I would get the hang of everything in no time at all and that all new mums are overwhelmed at the start. This made me feel a little bit better and I decided to ask a nurse to show me what to do the next time – after all how difficult could it actually be?

All that day the nurses kept trying to give David a bottle but to no avail. He refused to suck. By tea time they were getting concerned and called a doctor to take a look at him. They discovered he had no sucking reflex and he would have to be taken down to the neo-natal unit to give him fluids intravenously. I was upset but at the same time happy for the chance to rest and let someone else look after him. The following day I was feeling much better and was brought down to visit the baby. He was hooked up to the feeding tube and he looked so tiny and helpless. John and I had to wear white gowns and masks in order to enter the unit. We sat and watched as a nurse sat with David coaxing him to suck a little bit of milk from a bottle. Someone else was taking care of my baby. "This is not how it's supposed to be", that voice in my head was saying. It was a painstaking process, but eventually he was taking about a teaspoon of milk at a time. We were told he would have to stay in the unit until he was taking three fluid ounces at each feed. I had to go home without my baby! I was devastated and cried all the way home in the car. This was not going according to the plan! I felt like stamping my feet in frustration. I have a picture of myself taken at home that day, with an empty pram and a full glass of Baileys Irish Cream. I had given up all alcohol during the pregnancy, so if I couldn't have my baby home, I was going to have a very large glass of Baileys.

The next week involved several trips a day in to the hospital to sit with David, coaxing him to feed, and bit by bit the amount of milk he took increased, until eventually, nine days after he was born, we were allowed to take our baby home with us. I don't think I will ever forget that first day home with him. My lovely tidy house turned upside down in the space of a few minutes. Bottles, nappies, cots, sterilisers, blankets, bibs, presents, flowers, cards, spew, poo and wee; you name it, we were tripping over it. That lovely rocking chair I had dreamt of sitting on while bonding with my baby was covered in everything and anything. I couldn't have sat on it even if I had the time – I couldn't sit anywhere for 10 days! My mum who lived nearby came over to help get me organised. We eventually settled into a routine over the next couple of days: no sleep during the day, no sleep during the night – oh yes we had a routine all right.

The 18th of December was a day like any other until around four o'clock when a friend came to visit. We sat in the sitting room chatting for about an hour and during that time David took about half his bottle and fell asleep in his pram. Shortly after, my friend left, and I decided to get something ready for dinner. As I passed the sitting room door I looked in on David who was awake, and I decided to give him the rest of his bottle, as that would give me time to cook dinner and eat without being disturbed. I sat on the couch with him in the crook of my arm, feeding him. He guzzled away happily and, after a while, I stopped feeding him to let him get his wind up. I sat him up holding his little chin in my hand while I rubbed his back. No wind was coming up so I leaned him back into the crook of my arm again and that's when I noticed his colour. He was grey and floppy with a bluish tinge around his lips. My baby was dead! He wasn't breathing and I hadn't a clue what to do! I had read all the baby books but none of them mentioned this. I shook him gently in disbelief and then the adrenaline kicked in and I ran for the phone. Still holding him in one arm and shaking him gently, I dialled 999. I told them what had happened and they promised to send an ambulance straight away. Then I rang John, who was at work, simply saying: "Come home, there's something wrong with the baby". Poor John, he got an awful fright. Next I rang my mum who lived nearby and told her the same thing. All the time I was gently shaking David and praying for all I was worth – well not really saying prayers just repeating: "Oh God, oh God, oh God", over and over and over. I opened the front door and stood in the cold with the baby, who was dressed in just his sleep suit, waiting for someone to come and help. I have never in my life felt more inadequate than at that moment with my baby 'dead' in my arms and not having a clue what to do.

My mum was the first to arrive. When she reached the door she grabbed the baby and wrapped him in a blanket. She kept saying to me: "He's fine, he's fine, he moved a thumb, he's fine". Actually he hadn't moved at all and she too believed that he was dead.

The ambulance arrived next. The nurse ran in the driveway, grabbed the baby, pushed myself and my mum into the ambulance, and put the baby in my arms while she worked on him. From the window at the back of the ambulance I saw John arrive. My mother's dog had followed her over, so to prevent him being killed on the road, John grabbed him, shoved him in the car, and followed us to the hospital. So there was the ambulance with my Mum, myself, and the lifeless baby being followed by a terrified man and a dog in a car. I felt as if I had been propelled into a nightmare scene from a movie. I knew we were in trouble when the sirens were turned on and we drove through every red traffic light on our way to the hospital. I couldn't understand why the nurse was just tickling David's chest because that is what it looked like, but, I found out afterwards, she was trying to get his heart started again. There was no sound or response from the baby and when we reached the hospital the nurse took David from me and ran. We all followed in and sat in the corridor outside the room where they were working on him.

We sat outside, both of us wondering if the picture we had taken of him looking so tiny on the large couch in the sitting room would be the last one we would ever have of him. We were managing to hold it all together by talking about every subject under the sun as we waited for someone to come out and give us some news. Suddenly we heard it: a loud shrill cry of a baby, my baby. David was alive! I remember my knees buckling and I collapsed in a heap on the floor of the corridor. I was overwhelmed with relief. He was kept in the hospital for a couple of days to make sure he was ok and thank God he was. They diagnosed some problem with the part of the brain that kicks in to force us to take another breath being underdeveloped. They said it could happen again and so they trained us in CPR and advised us to get a baby monitor for him and that way we would be alerted by an alarm that would sound should he ever stop breathing again. He wore this for a year and it did go off regularly for the first four months but each time the alarm itself would jolt him into taking another breath. A week later we had David baptised in a rush as we felt afraid and unsure about everything at that stage.

One day blended into the next after that. David cried constantly, all day and all night. Every evening he threw up his bottle after his six pm feed. He would immediately take another bottle and keep that one down but would then scream and scream for almost four hours. The only thing we could do to calm him was put him in the car and drive. So that's what we did. Every night we drove around the town for hours to keep David quiet. One night, after about three months of this nightly drive, we were stopped at a Garda check point. The Garda shone his light into the back of the car and both of us hissed at him, like creatures from a horror film: "Don't wake the baby!" It was that or go insane at home, walking the floors with him, rolling him in the pram, and yet still he would scream and scream. I had a path beaten to the doctor's surgery thinking there must be something wrong with him. It could not be natural for a baby to scream for so long and so hard without there being something wrong with him! "Oh it's just colic", she said. "He'll grow out of it". "Yeah but when?" we were thinking. And were we going to survive much more of this?

One day in particular sticks out in my mind. David was crying all day. Nothing consoled him. I was exhausted. I was walking around the house with him in my arms just begging him to be quiet. I went upstairs to our bedroom and placed him in the middle of our bed and walked back to the door. There I looked back in at him, tears rolling down my face, and I roared at him: "shut up, just shut the f--k up!". Immediately I was grief stricken and ran and picked the little red faced bundle up off the bed. I rang my mum and asked her to come over. I finally admitted it. I couldn't do it all on my own. When John arrived home from work I told him I needed help with the baby. I needed a break. I needed some time for myself. "It's that or get him fostered", I told him, never more serious about anything in my life. I felt as if I was going out of my mind. Of course everyone was happy to help out. All I had to do was ask and I really did feel better able to cope once I got some time away on my own. Sometimes it was just a bath, a walk, or a cup of tea with a friend but those times saved my life and David's too probably, if the truth were told. When the colic eased we got into a more normal routine of sleep and feeds. At least for us it was normal. I didn't realise until I spoke to other mothers that getting up to your baby fifteen times a night was not normal. But that was what we were doing. We were both constantly tired in those days and to top it all I had to go back to work. David was only three months old. (In those days the maternity leave was very short). I went back on a part-time basis and the two Grannies shared the minding of David between them. No one else would take on the responsibility with the potential that he could stop breathing at a moment's notice. The arrangement worked really well and everyone was happy with the amount of time they had with the baby.

Now I knew I loved this little baby because after all he was mine and every mother loves their child – right? But it wasn't until one day when I was walking home from town wheeling David in his pram that I stopped and looked in at him for a moment. An overwhelming feeling of love came over me – I felt like a lion with a cub, fiercely protective of my little boy. It was in that moment, at the side of the road, three months after he was born, that I finally bonded with my baby.

I had never experienced anything like it in my life. It was all consuming and overwhelming. I felt so happy and in that moment knew things were going to be ok. We had been through so much with him in the first few months that I hadn't had the time to bond. I also believe that my body had not allowed me to bond with him because of the fear of him being taken from me.

From a very young age David showed his fiercely independent streak. He was never a cuddly baby. He always wanted to sit on our laps, facing out looking at the world. At four months he managed to move himself across the floor on one elbow. At ten months he started walking, and on his first birthday he was running around the house like a mad thing. At the age of three he sat on a couch in the sitting room, put his feet up on the coffee table and said: "I can't wait to have my own house – then I can put my feet where I want". Up to the age of two and a half David never slept a full night. He woke constantly in the night with a cough and eventually he was diagnosed with asthma. This meant he had to use a nebuliser several times a day. We had to sit with him holding a mask up to his face, as medicines to relieve the coughing were turned into a mist for him to inhale. This improved things greatly and he eventually started sleeping through the night - two weeks before his sister Laura was born!

Even though life with David as a young child was very difficult we had decided that we wanted to have a second child, so that David would have a companion growing up. A couple of weeks before I was due to give birth I was told that the baby was in the breach position but that everything was fine and I would be allowed to give birth naturally. Now I have to admit I was a bit freaked out at the idea of giving birth to a baby bottom or feet first and it didn't help when my father-in-law, who was from the country, said: "Sure don't cows give birth like that all the time". "I am not a cow", I wanted to roar at him. Nearer the time however, a scan revealed that the baby was actually in a very dangerous position for giving birth naturally and a decision was made that I would have a c-section. I was nervous about this but pleased that I was being spared the alternative. I went in to hospital on Thursday 27th May, 1993, and on the morning of 28th May I was brought down to the theatre to have my new baby. I had opted to be awake for the procedure which meant I had to have an epidural administered to numb me from the waist down. I don't know what I was expecting but the next thing I knew I was having my first ever panic attack. I couldn't breathe and I thought I was going to die. People were around me telling me to breathe slowly and deeply and that everything was fine. I heard the surgeon saying that if I didn't calm down I was to be "knocked out" (or words to that effect). I did calm down and a few minutes later my gorgeous baby girl was born. I just had enough time to register it was a girl when a mask was placed over my face and I knew no more. For some strange reason they decided it would be better if I was unconscious for the repair work. I never found out why I was anaesthetised at that stage of the process but the next thing I knew I was waking up in a hospital bed with everything over. I was very groggy and the nurses left me to sleep for a couple of hours. In the afternoon two nurses came to my bedside and told me that I needed to get up now and walk a bit. I was not in the mood for a walk but I allowed myself to be helped from the bed and on to the floor. Despite feeling as if my body had been cut in half, I might have actually been able to walk a little bit if I had legs. But I couldn't feel my legs. I could see them, I knew they were there, but couldn't feel a thing. I had a nurse on each side of me holding me up and trying to get me to walk. I was trying, I know I was, but it was no use. My two legs were just dragging along behind me and the nurses were getting frustrated. "Put your legs under you", one was saying. Suddenly a Staff Nurse appeared and started running down the corridor towards us: "Put that woman back into bed – she had an epidural". "Did you?" both of my nurses said in unison. At that stage all I could think was: 'Bed – great'. I was lifted off the ground by the two nurses and helped gingerly back in to bed and left there for many more hours.

I bonded immediately with this little girl, probably because I fed, and changed, and looked after her myself from the start. I was confident and knew what to do. After all I had plenty of experience at that stage so I wasn't nervous. She was a bigger baby than David had been and so I didn't feel as frightened of hurting her.

Two days later when I was feeling much stronger, John brought David in to see me and his new little sister. David was delighted with her and kept rubbing her little bald head. I was delighted to see him and his mischievous little grin. He climbed all over the bed and tore open the presents that 'Laura had brought from heaven for him'. A stuffed Ernie and Bert (from *Sesame Street*) that he had requested and which my poor mother had searched every shop for and eventually found when she was on holidays the week before Laura arrived.

A couple of days later I went home, this time with our new baby who took her bottle easily, slept, apart from when she needed to be fed or changed, and in general slotted in to our lives very easily.

As David had been the only child for two and half years, he did find it a bit difficult to share our time with this new little member of the family. He started to demand attention at the times when I was feeding Laura and this started to cause a little bit of friction. We took time to explain to him about how babies cannot feed themselves, we showed him pictures of him being fed as a baby, and we let him help in holding the bottle for Laura and generally included him as much as we could in the day to day care of her.

Life with the children was a roller coaster. Good days and not so good days. Days they got on well and days they fought like tigers. It was quite a 'normal' home with its ups and downs.

As I look back on those days, I feel as if I was simply a passenger in my life. Someone else had sat in to the driving seat and had taken over control. I seemed to no longer have a say in anything. Days blended into each other and life was hectic. Working, washing, ironing, cooking, cleaning, feeding, changing, playing, tidying – falling into bed exhausted.

Something had to give.

Chapter 4

The painful memories return

When I was thirty two years old and the kids were seven and five years old the reality of what had happened in my childhood came back to haunt me. I had been chatting with my sister when she mentioned, in a totally different context, the word 'manipulate'. I don't know exactly what happened but that word triggered a huge emotional outburst. I told her what Dad had done to me and I cried for hours. I think it must have been the fact that my own children were reaching the age I had been when the abuse began. My gorgeous daughter, full of fun and mischief, lovable, trusting and innocent, reminded me of what I must have been like when I was a child and I couldn't imagine hurting her for even a second. The pain was overwhelming. "Why now?" I asked myself. "I've been so great up until now." I had never forgotten the abuse but I had thought I was so strong that I was able to put it all behind me. The memories that came back caused an incredible blackness to descend on me. I cried and cried for the child I had been. I grieved for the childhood I had lost. I grieved for the person I could have been without these awful things happening to me. I couldn't stop thinking about the kind of life I would be leading if all the bad stuff hadn't happened. I felt as if I was in the movie 'Sliding Doors'. One life was with the abuse and the other was without. Why couldn't I have had the other life? I was very angry and found it incredibly difficult to deal with the intensity of my anger. For weeks and weeks I cried whenever I was alone. I put on a brave face for my husband and the kids, but inside I felt as if my heart was breaking with the sadness and the pain. I couldn't understand it. Why me? What had I done to deserve this? I couldn't understand how I had kept quiet? All it would have taken was one word in the right ear. Was it my fault? Why didn't I tell somebody? Did I need to feel special so badly? Was it that I craved love so deeply that I kept my mouth shut? Had I wanted it to happen? Did I enjoy the excitement of it all, the one being singled out? I was angry at myself for not speaking up, for not telling a teacher, a friend a neighbour or even my own Mum. I couldn't understand how I had been manipulated into staying quiet. What had I been afraid of? The questions went on and on in my head. The confusion was incredible. My head felt as if it was going to explode. As the weeks went on the pain became worse and worse. I was finding it difficult to cope with the thoughts in my head. I began to find myself in a very dark place with thoughts I wasn't able to deal with. When one day my thoughts became very dark I knew I was in trouble and needed help so I sought out a counsellor. I was unlucky with who I chose. During the hour-long sessions the counsellor kept trying to get me to blame my mother for the whole thing, for not protecting me. I got worse instead of better. Each session involved going over and over what had happened and the pain got worse and worse. One day I decided I had had enough. I realised the road I was on was not helping me. I was reliving all the pain again and arguing with the counsellor about whether or not my mother was to blame. I had to go over and over all the pain from those times. Now I know there are really excellent counsellors out there and it can be a very beneficial way to deal with trauma but I was just really unlucky with the one I chose.

I later discovered when I went on to train as a therapist myself that the brain doesn't know the difference between what is real and what is imagined. If, for example, you close your eyes and imagine yourself lying on a beach in the sun with the sand between your toes and the sound of the waves crashing in the distance, the heat of the sun on your face, your body will respond as if it is actually there. You will feel warm and relaxed as if you are on holidays. Similarly when I went back over the abuse again and again, my body and mind responded as if I was going through the experiences again and I felt horrible. There had to be an easier way. I phoned the counsellor to tell her I would not be going back and she told me that I was making a big mistake: it would all come back to haunt me at some time in the future if I didn't keep going with the counselling now. I decided to take the risk.

I thought about the situation I was in and decided to sit and feel the pain for a while and really try to understand what I was feeling. Instead of feeling overwhelmed and angry, I decided to find out what these feelings were about. Instead of someone else telling me what they were, I decided to go inside myself and see exactly what was going on. What, throughout the years, had I been afraid of feeling? What did that little girl inside me want to say? What pain was buried deep inside me? I knew that I had been wearing a mask for a long time and I had built a wall around myself pretending the feelings weren't there so that I could get on with my life. But those feelings were in there and now was the time to find out what they were.

I really had had enough of feeling bad. I wanted to feel happy and good about myself again. I was determined to find a way to do this. I sat down one day and thought about what was going on inside my head. I decided to examine closely each of the questions that was screaming at me from inside. I needed to know why I was feeling so bad. Why was I so angry? What had I needed as a child that had been missing? The answers came to me as I took the time to ask myself the questions and listen to the answers. A lot of realisations came to me as I gave this time to myself to be still and to listen.

I was hurt and I was very angry. I was confused and torn between love and hate. I looked at my own children and wondered how a parent could do something like that to an innocent child. The pain in my body was immense. It felt like my guts were being twisted and a cold steel knife was in my heart. I didn't know how I was going to get out of this but I was determined that I would. I knew I couldn't go back to the time where I had been pretending everything was fine and so the only way was through this and out the other side, wherever that would lead to.

And so I sat and I thought and I thought. And I cried and I cried and I cried as all the feelings came up. I was angry that I hadn't been safe in my own home, in my own bed. I knew the effort I made to look after my children, and now I began to realise that I did not feel safe when I was alone with my Dad. What a realisation this was. What an awful way for a child to feel. I was constantly afraid of that call from the window when I was sitting on my swing. I used to keep my head down and pretend not to see him beckoning to me but eventually I would look up and, as if I was hypnotised, I would go to him. This made me angry and really sad for that little girl. Every child deserves to feel safe in her own home. If not there, then where?

I was angry at myself for not speaking up – I was cross with myself for being so weak, for not telling somebody who would listen and do something about it. I told myself it was my own fault, then it was his, then it was mine again. The confusion was intense. As I felt all the anger, really felt it and understood where it was coming from, it started to ease and then there was more confusion as the next emotion came up.

I remembered that there was a weird sense of excitement that infiltrated the sense of monotony around school and music lessons and I thought that this may have had something to do with why I didn't say anything. I had a secret that nobody knew about and it felt a little like the Enid Blyton *Famous Five* books that I loved. I knew something no one else did. And I couldn't tell – couldn't tell anyone at all or my Daddy would die. Children's minds work in mysterious ways and as I recognised the part I played in the whole thing (unintentionally I must add) - I recognised that I was feeling very guilty. Guilty for letting it go on and not shouting out loud the very first time it happened. I blamed myself and it was good to acknowledge that these were feelings that were very real for me.

I knew for definite that it had made me feel special. I was being singled out from the others. I know this seems strange, but I remembered that as the middle child, being neither the eldest nor the youngest nor the only boy, I felt as if I didn't really have a place in the family. I felt my place as the youngest member of the family had been taken by my younger sister and I never really felt that I fitted in after that. The abuse in some way made up for it. I was special again. I was told that it was time to be a big girl now because my little sister was the baby. Was this what it meant to be a big girl? As I felt all these feelings, the sadness I felt for the little girl inside me was immense, that need to feel special being met in such an awful way. I felt that pain for a very long time. I shed lots of tears as that sadness welled up inside me to be acknowledged. I felt a deep sadness to my very core and the sobs that came from that place made me feel as if I was falling apart.

And I remembered being afraid. I remembered being afraid to go to sleep until he was gone to bed. I was on alert all the time, not knowing when or where. I went right back to some of the times when I felt most afraid; when I realised I was alone in the house with him and that I couldn't leave. I could feel it like a scream in my throat that wanted to come out. Fear that was just bottled up inside with no way of being expressed. I felt the fear of having no control over what was going to happen next. And that led to me feeling more anger. And I sat and felt that anger and acknowledged to myself how angry I felt at having no control over this situation.

I needed to be loved and in some strange way I felt loved by him. He bought me things when events upset me a lot and he was afraid I was going to tell. One time he bought me a really pretty skirt and t-shirt. This made me happy. I liked pretty things. Other times I got extra pocket money. He often said he was sorry to me and he often told me that he loved me and this was how he showed it. I liked being told that I was loved. Sometimes he cried; I remember him getting upset and promising it would never happen again, and I would comfort him telling him it was ok. This made me feel special too, being able to bring comfort to somebody.

I felt so hurt that he knew how to win me over and used that against me. I sat in that feeling for a long time, feeling the pain and the hurt at being used.

As I went back through my childhood and acknowledged all the feelings associated with it, I learned a lot.

I learned what had been important to me as a child. I needed to be free of fear in my home. I needed to feel safe. I needed some excitement in my life to break the monotony. I needed to feel that I mattered; that I was important. I needed Love.

As I pondered on my childhood and the things I needed, what was missing and how the abuse had in some way given me what I needed, I started to think: "If I needed these things as a child, then my children must need them too". I hadn't been aware of what my children actually needed in their life up until this point. We had just been drifting along, as I said earlier, more like passengers in our lives rather than the drivers, doing what came naturally and assuming we were doing ok.

Many people think it is very strange that abuse victims don't tell anyone what has happened them in their childhood until they are in their thirties, forties or even older.

You may be wondering this yourself. The reason this happens is that our unconscious mind, the part of us that stores our emotions and our memories, wants to protect us. It sometimes keeps painful memories and emotions buried until we reach a time in our lives when we have the ability to work through them, heal from them and move on. If you are finding old painful memories resurfacing, rest assured that you now have what it takes to face them head on and let them go.

I had never forgotten what had happened but I had pushed it away and told myself I was a really strong person to have coped so well. What I discovered was I had pushed it away because I was so afraid that I wouldn't be able to deal with the depth of the emotion involved. However I learned that now I could. My emotions are there to help me express what I am feeling and once I do this it becomes easier to let the old feelings go and move on with my life. Nothing can be as bad as the experience itself, so I know that the traumatic events are over now and all I am doing is beginning to release emotions that are buried deep inside me.

The other thing I learned is that emotions that are buried can play havoc with our physical bodies. All through my twenties I was plagued with one illness after the other: appendicitis, scarlet fever, constant recurring tonsillitis and the most serious being a virus in my heart that left me extremely ill.

It was time for a change.

CHAPTER 5

THE JOURNEY BEGINS

This was the start of my new journey. I remember standing in my kitchen one day preparing dinner and saying to myself: "That's it, I am not going to spend one more day feeling sorry for myself or being angry about this. There has to be something I can do". I knew I could not change the past no matter how much counselling I went to – talking about it was not going to change what happened and so I made a decision to turn all the negative things in my childhood into good. I was going to make sure that my kids felt safe, special and loved. I was going to make sure that they had all the important things that I felt had been missing in my childhood.

I also realised that I still needed these things. Just because I was older didn't mean I no longer needed to feel love. I did and I realised that I didn't have to wait for or depend on someone else to give it to me either. It was lovely to receive love from someone else and I could love myself too.

I began by being kind to myself by accepting myself exactly as I was. There was a good reason why in that moment I felt broken. I had been through a lot and I had built that wall up to protect myself because I knew no better. I had been so afraid to feel exactly what was inside that I had pushed it away. *I had been afraid that I couldn't handle the depth of emotion inside me. I had been afraid that I would 'go over the edge' or 'crack up' if I allowed myself to feel all those feelings inside.* But I had reached the stage where those feelings needed to be felt and I had survived. I began to feel compassion for myself and what I had been through. I was beginning to understand myself and accept myself. The worst had happened, the volcano had erupted, and I had coped. And now I started to feel a little excited because I didn't know what was going to come next. Who was I, now that I had taken all this old emotional garbage out and looked at it? The realisation that I needed certain things in my life, and my kids did too, began a whole new journey for me. I started by being kinder to myself and being more gentle with myself. I took time out to walk, meet friends, go to exercise classes and I also began to go to night classes studying different things that appealed to me. I found that when I treated myself lovingly I felt better and I could do it any time I chose. I didn't have to wait for someone else to do something to make me feel good. I could make myself feel good by doing more things that made me happy. I had never paid any attention to what these things were but the more in tune with myself that I became the more obvious they became.

I acknowledged to myself what a strong woman I am. I have amazing strength and I now knew how to be the best mum I could possibly be. I felt as if I had been given an instruction book for raising my kids. I had been given the secret to successfully raising kids to be happy, self-confident, loving adults.

As I stood in the kitchen that day I felt a surge of powerful and determined energy surge through my body as that decision was made. I was taking back my power. I was not going to let my childhood mean that I spent the rest of my life grieving and angry for something that was taken away from me. I knew that wasn't the kind of mum I wanted my kids to have. I wasn't going to let another generation suffer as a result of my experiences.

But where to start? Well the first thing I knew was that even though I had acknowledged all these feelings deep inside me they hadn't gone away. I knew that if I thought about those times I could still feel those old feelings. At that time I didn't know that this was something that could be released from my system; that I could remove those old emotions that came up whenever I thought of those times. That was something I was going to discover later on when I worked with a therapist to release all the old fear, anger, sadness, hurt and guilt associated with my childhood and I feel truly blessed to be able to do this now with my own clients.

I decided to focus on my children and the life I wanted to create for my family. I had felt a huge release after acknowledging the pain inside me. For too long I had pushed it down hoping that if I pushed hard enough, it would never come out.

This was an opportunity to show my children what you can do when you make up your mind to do it: choosing to take responsibility for yourself instead of staying in a victim mentality. Later, when they were older, I would share my experiences with them. You have a choice. You always have a choice. I could choose to go under, drink, or take drugs to take the pain away, and I would have had the perfect excuse. *Everyone would understand why and I could be excused for not making a go of things. But was that what I wanted? Did I want that excuse or did I want to be the absolutely best mum that I could possibly be?* Being a fantastic mum sounded more like what I wanted and that's the road I took. I rescued myself.

The journey began as I started to think about all the things that were really important to me about my family. I thought back to the dreams I had as a child about the family I wanted to have. There had to be lots of love and fun. I wanted them to have a strong sense of belonging to a unit like they had in 'Little House on the Prairie'. I wanted to be able to talk to my children and I wanted them to be able to talk to me about things going on in their lives. I wanted them to trust me and I wanted a peaceful and happy home. Respect for each other and honesty were important to me too. I wanted there to be forgiveness, as I knew the damage that could be done by holding on to bitterness and resentment. I knew that if I focused on ensuring that all these things existed within *this* family, then we would go a long way to becoming the kind of family I wanted and I would feel happier.

The next question was: "How do I do this, what kind of mum do I need to become?" Honestly, I hadn't a clue. But I began to think and look at others who I perceived to be normal mothers. I read books, watched movies and TV programmes, and began to copy what other people were doing, people who appeared to have the kind of family life I wanted.

I wanted us to be able to talk to each other about everything so I began to think about what I needed to do and what kind of mum I needed to be to make sure that we could all talk to each other.

Peace, joy and fun were important to me so I needed to find out what kind of Mum I needed to be to make sure that this happened.

These were the kind of questions I began to ask myself. And then, little by little, I chose to become the kind of mum who believed these things were important. I began to think about how this Mum would act, how she would speak, how she would feel, what she would do and what she would look like.

I started off by pretending I was the kind of mum I wanted to be. It was as if I put on a Magic Coat and, when I was wearing it, I could be exactly what I wanted to be: full of love, joy and fun. I played games and was relaxed and happy. I kissed, cuddled and played with the kids. When I wore that 'coat' I came up with lots of ideas on how to talk with the kids and how to show them what respect and forgiveness were all about. I discovered ways to create a sense of belonging for the kids. When I wore this coat I was free and able to have fun, do silly things and not care what anyone thought.

It was magic.

The interesting thing was that, as I wore this Coat and behaved the way the mum I wanted to be behaved, I gradually found I didn't need that Coat anymore. I had become her: the mum with magic kisses.

Chapter 6

The Magic

It's true that you can't change the past – I was never going to be able to change what happened to me. What you can do though is decide how you are going to let it affect you. You can have the attitude of "poor me" and keep telling yourself the same story over and over again about how awful it was, or you can decide to use what you know to make a difference in your children's lives. That is what I decided to do: use the knowledge I had to make sure that my kids grew up in a home where they felt cherished and loved and, in the beginning, that was all I thought I would get out of it – a sense of satisfaction that at least my kids had a happy childhood.

However, what I went on to discover was something absolutely magical. *As I loved them and cared for them, played with them and read to them, as I told them how much I loved them, kissed them and cuddled them - each time I looked at their happy little faces, a little piece of me healed.* Every time I hugged them and their little arms tightened around my neck, another wound disappeared. As I became a mum full of love for my children and doing my best for them, the feelings I had from the lack of love in the past disappeared and I began to heal.

My pain came from the feeling of the absence of love in my childhood, but when my heart filled with love for my children that love healed me. When I had been angry and bitter the wounds got worse. When I held on to resentment and blame I felt overwhelmed and out of control. When I focused on loving myself, my husband, and my kids, and gave them what they needed, a miracle happened. My pain started to go away.

As I gave the kids what I had needed as a child I noticed that I gradually became more and more content. As I loved them, I rose above the lack of love in my past. It no longer held me back. Instead it seemed to propel me forward, making me strong and filling that void that had been inside for such a long time.

CHAPTER 7

TAKE MY HAND

You may be a new mum, a mum with one or two or more kids, you may have had a fantastic childhood or one that you felt was lacking in some or even many ways. You may have given some thought as to the kind of parent you want to be, and you may not have given it any thought at all, and just decided to trust your instincts, or you may be just sailing along hoping and trusting that everything turns out ok.

I often hear mums say they wish that kids came with a "user manual". You get instructions when you buy a washing machine and yet, with something as precious as a human being, there's nothing.

My kids are twenty two and twenty four now and I have entered a new phase with them. We have a lovely relationship where we enjoy spending time together and time apart. Family has always been important to us and I hope it always is. We still make the effort to get us all together from time to time, and I think it's nice that they know that, even though their lives are moving on and changing, we will always be Team Collins.

The following chapters are written from my memories of raising the kids, how my new way of being a parent helped them, the difference it made in our home, and at the end are the kids' own thoughts on the type of childhood they had: how they felt and how they feel their childhood contributed to their being the adults they are today.

What started out as a desire to create a different childhood for my kids turned out to be my journey of healing and the discovery that I really **did** have magic kisses. With effort and determination to create a home filled with love and happiness I discovered a power that we all have within us. **_The power to choose what happens next in our lives._**

I couldn't change the past but I went on to create a very happy life afterwards. I learned so much over the years. I didn't always get it right. There were times when I screamed at the kids, times when we fell out, times when I was too tired to give them what they needed. I wasn't a perfect mother. My kids had tantrums that embarrassed me, I didn't always cook a well-balanced dinner for them and there were times when I was not the kind of mum I wanted to be. Sometimes I was hard on myself and other times I was maybe too easy on myself. Being a parent is a journey with good days and bad days but when I made decisions based on the love I had for my family I knew I couldn't go wrong.

If you have been hurt as a child I ask you to give this a shot. It worked for me and I know it can work for you too. Please, let me show you the way. I know what it's like to feel pain. I know the sense of being overwhelmed that sometimes takes over. I know the sadness that can be buried so deep you don't think you can ever get over it. I know that feeling of wanting to curl up in a ball and make everything go away. I've been there. You may be thinking it's easy for me to say all this but what have you to lose by giving it a go? You have everything to gain though.

Our kids depend on us for everything. They trust us to take care of them. When they fall they know a kiss from us can make everything better. Our kisses are magic because they come from love. If you feel you don't have that magic inside, I'll show you step by step how to find it, and how to show it, and very soon you will know what you have always known: you are the magic your kids need.

All Mums and Dads have the magic kisses their children need. You just need the determination and the desire to find them....

Before I start please remember that this is what *I* did. I'm not a psychologist – I'm sure there was a better way to deal with some of the

38

issues I came across. I wasn't and am not perfect, so treat what you read here as signposts. If you try something and it doesn't work for you, please go ahead and try something else. Be flexible. What worked with my kids might not work with yours. As long as the intention is clear you will find the path that is right for you and your family. The important thing is to remember what it is you are trying to achieve and to keep trying a mixture of different things until you achieve it.

CHAPTER 8

THE WARM FUZZY FEELING

When David and Laura were born they were helpless babies looking to me and my husband for their every need to be met. We wanted them to feel safe and secure in the knowledge that we would always be there for them to give them what they needed. In the beginning they needed us for everything and as they grew up they needed us less and less. Now they rarely need us for anything except to chat about things going on in their lives and maybe to look for some advice now and then.

It was really important to me that they grew up feeling safe and protected. Because of what happened to me I knew how important that was. I wanted something different for them.

So, of course, we fed them when they were hungry, kept them warm and dry, and looked after them when they hurt themselves or got upset.

And there was so much more I found I could do.

I loved tucking them up in bed at night, kissing them goodnight, filling their tummies with good wholesome food, tickling them and enveloping them in hugs that let them know they were totally and utterly loved. When they cried we went to them. If they needed our arms around them they got them. We let them know we were there to take care of them and make sure they were ok.

Holding their hands when we were outside until the time came that they had enough road sense for us to let go meant we went at their pace not ours. They would often pull us to look more closely at something and holding their hands gave them the courage to explore, with us there to protect them. They felt safe investigating new things. As they investigated I began to see things in a different way too. I noticed again the wonder of a cobweb in the frost, a daisy, cracks on the pavement, a kitten under a car and ladybirds. All the things I had forgotten about as I grew older took on new meaning for me. Our kids slowed us down so that we could experience each moment for what it was, full of joy and wonder, with them.

Every day we asked them about their day: we were interested in them and we let them know they could talk to us about anything. They were able to tell us if they had got into trouble at school, forgotten to do homework, had a fight with somebody, or had been caught talking in class. Naturally we sometimes felt the urge to express our disapproval of how they had behaved, and indeed sometimes we did so, but we always did our best to listen and let them talk about how they felt about what happened. It was more important that they were able to keep telling us about what was going on in their lives than it was to get our own viewpoint heard on what we felt they should have done. We wanted them to feel safe telling us everything. For if they didn't feel safe talking to us, then who would they ever feel safe talking to?

Listening to them ensured they understood that what they had to say was important. I wanted to be certain that when the time came when they might need to speak up they would have the confidence and the ability to do so.

And so we listened to the endless stories of who did what at school.

We listened to how awful it was that they couldn't play outside at school because it was raining.

We listened to the debate on whether shoes or sandals should be worn today.

We listened to the arguments about which movie should be watched and why.

We listened to how sore an invisible cut was.

And we heard:

That a bus driver made an inappropriate approach on the way home from school.

That a child was upset because someone had been unkind to him.

That a child was afraid of a teacher.

That a child was sad and thought he was stupid because of a note from a teacher in a homework notebook.

That a child was feeling left out in a group of friends.

As a result, I have seen them speak up when they felt someone was being treated unfairly, or had been wrongly accused of something; also when they did not want to succumb to peer pressure and engage in vandalism for example and when they felt they were not being heard at home.

My face did and still does light up when I see them and I always let them know I am pleased to see them. I took notice of them and let them know I loved them and enjoyed being with them.

Giving them this warm fuzzy feeling of being safe helped them have an amazing start in life: they believe they can do and be anything they want to be. Growing up feeling safe means they trust and believe that life is good and that good things will happen to them. They have the confidence to know that they can handle anything that comes their way. They are eager to learn and to trust. In general they are generous, relaxed and happy young adults.

There is no doubt that raising kids was a daunting prospect. These little people looked to us to raise them to be happy and successful adults and, in the beginning we hadn't a clue how to do it. Our only experience of parenting was our own parents and we wanted to do some things the same and other things different. How many times have we said to ourselves; "Oh God, I sound just like my mother or father"? We vowed we would never say the things they said such as: "While you're under this roof etc. etc.", "Because I said so" and so on. These are the only experiences we have had so they are what we were inclined to fall back on sometimes.

When the kids were small I worried about whether or not I was doing things 'right'. Being a mum felt like a huge responsibility. I was hard on myself, telling myself I could do better. I was critical of myself if I shouted at them or became impatient. And then I remembered the sleepless nights comforting and feeding them, the hours spent kissing sore knees, putting plasters on fingers, driving to friend's houses, standing in the rain outside the school to collect them – all the things a mum does and I became kinder to myself.

Looking back, these are the key things I feel we did to give them that warm fuzzy feeling:

We were in charge.

We set limits.

We spent lots of time together.

We ensured they were free from fear and physical pain.

We met their emotion with emotion – not logic.

There were consequences to their actions.

We had lots of routines.

We made sure they knew we loved them.

Now, let's look at each of those in greater detail:

We were in charge.

I quickly realised that my dream of being my kids' best friend was not going to work. Someone had to be in charge because these children needed someone they could depend on. They might not always like the decisions we made or understand them but they could relax at being kids with us at the wheel. When we are on a plane we don't want the pilot sitting down beside us freaking out at a bit of turbulence. We want him in the cockpit taking care of us, knowing what he is doing and staying super cool and calm. This then instils a sense of calm in us and we know everything is going to be ok. We did our best to remain calm when they had tantrums, got in trouble or lost their temper. We wanted them to have the comfort of knowing that we were capable of guiding them through the difficult times they were experiencing. We made sure they knew we were in charge of the household. We set the limits. We were the parents and when they were small we decided what was best for them. We ensured that they didn't have to worry about anything that they could do nothing about, and made sure they knew we were there taking care of them. We kept worries away from them unless they directly affected them and even then we let them know that we were taking care of the problem. They knew they could rely on us for what they needed.

We set limits.

Teaching and guiding the kids involved setting limits. Just a few of them were:

We encouraged them to be kind to each other and didn't allow them to hit each other.

We didn't tolerate bad language.

We taught them to say please and thank you at appropriate times.

We reminded them that certain behaviour can cause damage to themselves, someone else or to a relationship with someone. Letting them see the effect of their behaviour helped them to avoid bad behaviour for a reason other than that they might get punished.

I had been raised a Roman Catholic but very little of it resonated with me. At a very deep level, however, I knew there was something greater than ourselves and beneath the pain and hurt lay a strong desire to feel and show love for myself and others. I wasn't sure how to instil this in the kids but I discovered a very simple way that they still use today. I simply asked them to "treat others as they would like to be treated". Then when one of them did something to hurt another we asked them to put themselves in the other person's shoes and see how they would feel if they were treated that way.

When Laura was about eight years old she was invited to a birthday party and she had accepted the invitation. A couple of days later she got an invitation to another party that sounded like a lot more fun (they were having a disco) and it was taking place on the same day as the one for which she had accepted the invitation. She really wanted to go to the second party and was in a quandary as to what she should do. I got her to imagine she was that first friend organising the party and imagine how she would feel if someone decided to go to a different party instead. Straight away she decided to go to the first party even though she was very disappointed about not going to the second.

This simple thing I taught them helped them to tune in and feel, for themselves, the decision that felt right for them to make.

I have come across many clients who simply cannot make decisions. People who keep looking to others for their opinion on what they should do. **Teaching our kids to make decisions was an invaluable skill.** Now they didn't always make the decision we would have liked or thought was right and we often tried to guide them, but when they made a decision they had to live with the consequences. *We helped them to take responsibility for their actions all the time by talking things out with them and listening to them*. Rather than telling them what to do we encouraged them to make decisions for themselves. This ability to make decisions for themselves has been very useful to them as they have got older and begun their own lives as adults.

There were some things that were very important for the kids to learn. Like if they hurt somebody, or forgot to feed the dog, it was important for them to see that they had caused pain, and in this way they were more likely to avoid doing the same thing in the future. There were other things that were less important and although it wasn't easy to bite my tongue and say nothing, I did my best. Like if they went out to play without a jacket even though I had asked them to put one on, I would do my best to say nothing and hope that next time they went out they would remember they were cold the last time and wear it. In this way they learnt to take responsibility for themselves. It was important to me that we focused on the things that really mattered.

One of the things that I found difficult as they got older was if they were late home from a friend's house or school or from a school trip. I would worry that something had happened to them. I knew that the reason they had not made contact was that they were probably so caught up with their pals that they weren't even thinking. One day I sat them down and I explained to them how I felt when they did this. I told them how much I loved them and that when I didn't hear from them I was concerned. I told them that I didn't need a long phone call - a simple text message letting me know they were ok was all I needed. When they put themselves in my shoes they thought differently about it and after that they usually remembered and I often got a message simply saying "I'm alive". They didn't really understand why I worried, after all they may have just been at a friend's house but they accepted that I did worry and usually sent the text.

We spent lots of time together.

We made sure to spend lots of time together as a family and this helped develop all of us into a strong unit. During the week when we were working and the kids were in school, this time together mostly consisted of having dinner together in the evenings. We nearly always sat down to the table together and this was an opportunity for everyone to chat about their day. John and I sat at each end of the table which was against a wall and the kids sat beside each other. In this way each parent was able to talk to one child easily and also encourage the eating of vegetables!

Looking back I think this was one of the reasons our family became a very strong unit. Everyone went out during the day but regrouped in the evenings. This created a strong sense of belonging in the kids. I'm sure this sense of belonging at home contributed to them being able to make up their own mind about whether or not to join in with things their peer groups were doing. They didn't crave a sense of belonging because they had it already.

Around the table was where we planned the weekend activities, talked about school and how they were getting along. We also spoke about our day and shared funny stories. The kids told the jokes they had heard in school and of course we all laughed even when Laura's joke at one stage was the same one each evening for months:

"Knock knock,

Who's there?

Orange.

Orange who?

Orange orange.

Mmmmm......"

She would be in fits of laughter trying to tell it and we would laugh at the spluttering and her thinking that the joke was hilarious. It was light-hearted and fun, most of the time. But, of course, we weren't *The Waltons*, so there were evenings when people were tired and cranky. Kids refused to eat, kids were fighting and grumpy, or one of us was tired and cranky and those evenings were not very pleasant and ended quickly. We were a family like any other. We found some days more difficult than others but our goal all the time was to have this special time together in the evenings. Sometimes it worked, sometimes it didn't but there was always tomorrow.

Now, I was no Jamie Oliver (I've improved over the years) but I could make a great Spaghetti Bolognese with salad; fish fingers, potato waffles and beans (when I was tired); heated up left overs (always on a Monday) and a few other quick and easy meals which was all I needed. There were lots of easy, healthy ways of serving up dinner and the important thing was that we all sat down without one of us being exhausted from slaving over a kitchen stove.

The evenings could be a very stressful time and they were especially stressful in the early days when I went back to working full time when the kids were about eight and ten years old. One day I came home after a really bad day at work. I was stressed, cranky, and cross and I remember coming in the door and they were simply bursting to tell me their stories about school. I remember not really listening to them and being more concerned about how I was going to tackle the pile of work I had to face the next day. I remember catching sight of myself in the mirror and wondering what was going on here. Being a mum was really important to me; I always wanted to hear about their day because I knew it was important that the kids got to share all the bits and pieces that had happened. I stopped for a moment and started to think about how I could leave work behind when I came home so that I could be fully there with the kids. I needed to come home and be mum instead of this stressed out person I was turning into.

The following day on my way home from work I pulled in to a petrol station about half a mile from home for 10 minutes – I stopped and started thinking. I realised that I had numerous things to do with work going around and around in my head. I found a pen and a piece of paper and wrote down each of the things that were taking up space in my head. I could now forget about them until the following day because there was nothing more I could do at this point about them. I imagined myself with two different hats. One was my work hat and one was my Mum hat. I pictured myself taking off my work hat, putting it on the back seat with the list of things for work, and I then put on my Mum hat. I told myself I could pick up the other hat and the list the following morning. The ten minutes spent 'changing hats' made a huge difference to me and the family. It meant that when I came in the door at home I was Mum.

At the weekend we spent more time together, there were trips to the market, walks in the woods, swimming or all of us cycling together. We had four bikes and became a regular sight on the roads around our area.

We ensured they were free from fear and physical pain.

We made sure the kids were never afraid for their physical safety. We never hurt them. There were no exceptions to this.

We met their emotion with emotion – not logic.

Were you ever really upset about something, and when you told a friend or partner about it, they tried to talk you around telling you all the reasons why there was no need for you to feel that way? How did that feel? Did it help? Would a simple hug or "Oh that's terrible – you must be feeling really sad" have helped more? I know if I am upset I just want someone to listen and understand why I am upset. I don't want them to solve a problem or try to make it all go away unless I specifically ask for that. Kids are the same. We found when we made the effort to listen to why they were upset and let them cry or give out about it they felt better quicker. *It was really important that we understood what they were feeling even if we didn't really understand why. A big hug and a "tell me about it" were often all they needed. This helped them to understand their own feelings. I know a lot of adults who have never learned to understand and get in touch with what they are feeling. They often think it is too painful a place to go –that they may be overwhelmed if they do. A lot of people turn to food, cigarettes and alcohol to avoid having to feel. We found that letting the kids express what they were feeling and helping them to understand why they were feeling that way helped them grow up being able to express themselves very clearly.* Yes, this meant they expressed their anger as well as all the other emotions, and when we listened and really heard why they were angry it soon abated, and we were able to discuss what was really going on for them. I know that if we had said to them: "Control your temper, come back when you've calmed down" and so on, they would probably have felt patronised and would be less inclined to express it in the future. We have emotions for a reason. They are an inner guide for us and they help us make decisions. If we were to tell the kids not to feel a certain way we would have being doing them a huge disservice. We found letting them express whatever emotion they were feeling helped them to process whatever was happening in their lives at the time.

There were consequences to their actions.

As we live in a world where there are always consequences to our actions, we recognised that the kids needed to learn this. We know, as adults, if we break the law we will be punished. We can't do whatever we want. It was our job as parents to teach this to the kids from the start. We felt we needed to teach this very early on as it would probably have been very difficult to teach this to them later on in life. We considered it our job as parents to teach them how to be able to go out into the world and get along with other people, earn a living, have relationships and be happy. Letting the two of them know from the start what was acceptable behaviour and what was not, was one of the ways we showed them we loved them. A badly behaved toddler can seem cute sometimes but it's not so cute when they get older. Our goal was to get them thinking for themselves and recognise when something they were doing was hurting someone else. Sometimes, of course, despite reasoning with them, they would carry on misbehaving.

I found this difficult and it very often hurt me as much as them to enforce these consequences if they misbehaved. There was one day when David was about six or seven years old that really sticks out in my mind. He kept hitting the furniture with his fire engine. I gave him a warning that if he didn't stop, I would take his red fire engine that he had only recently received as a birthday present, and I would put it away where he couldn't see it for a time. Well, he just would not stop, so I took the fire engine and walked up the stairs with it to put it up high in a wardrobe. My heart was breaking as he was behind me crying and saying over and over: "I'm sorry Mammy, I'm sorry Mammy. Please don't take it away". I believed that he was only saying sorry because I was actually doing what I had said I would do, and I also knew that if I gave in and gave it back he would get the message that if you accidentally push too far you can get out of it by crying and begging. I felt it would not have been the right message to give him. Even though it broke my heart to do it I knew I had to. This was a difficult part of parenting – we loved them so much and showing that love often involved doing things that were difficult.

When the time was up he simply got the toy back. There was no big deal made of it. I always wanted them to feel good about themselves so this was just about teaching them that there were consequences to all their actions.

We had lots of routines.

Having routines gave the children a sense of security and also helped them to develop self-discipline. A big fear we as human beings have is "fear of the unknown". The kids were exposed to change on a daily basis. They were introduced to new people, new foods, they had to learn new skills, they had to learn to share and make new friends. They got new teachers at school, David got a new sibling and their bodies were changing all the time. Having a predictable routine at home helped them to cope with all this change.

Having predictable routines allowed the kids to feel safe. They then learnt to cope with bigger and bigger changes in their lives. When the kids felt safe they developed confidence in their abilities, and so, step by step, they started to take on new things like walking to a friend's house by themselves, buying something in a shop or staying over at a friend's house. Sometimes unpredictable things happened in their lives. A best friend moved away, Mum or Dad had to go away on business or a relative died. The kids experienced the death of a grandparent when David was six and Laura was three. Laura was too young to know the difference but David was very upset. He was afraid of who was going to leave his life next. He needed lots of reassurance and to the best of our ability at the time we maintained the routines that we had in place. He was a bit anxious, but by us making his days as predictable as possible, he gradually began to realise that all was ok again in his world.

The more routines there were in their lives the more safe and secure they felt. This didn't mean that the routines were written in stone. Far from it – *a lot of the joy in having routines was occasionally breaking them* - like staying up late to watch the *Late Late Toy Show*, having a movie night and the kids going to bed at the same time as us, not clearing up after dinner because a friend had called over, or staying up for a birthday party. I can remember a couple of times someone getting a longing for a bag of chips and there was a trip to town when they should have been going to bed and we drove around town eating them. The kids loved this and I can remember them chatting about how their friends were all probably in bed and they were out in the dark eating chips. It was such a simple thing but I can still remember the grins in the back of the car, the smell of salt and vinegar and that lovely warm feeling of doing something a bit different from the norm.

Having routines made life easier for everyone and the kids learnt a skill that they took with them into adulthood – how to put structure around their own lives.

Some of the routines we had were:

Going to bed at the same time every night.

Brushing teeth before bed and in the morning.

Getting the schoolbags ready the night before school.

Eating dinner at the table each evening.

Reading them a story every night.

Getting homework done before dinner.

We found there was an enormous benefit to having routines. We didn't have to nag as much because brushing teeth, getting schoolbags ready, and so on, just became what we did at that time of day. There wasn't a choice as to whether you did it or not. It reduced stress on everybody and because of that there was usually a nice atmosphere in the house.

We did our best to keep in mind that we were preparing our children to go out into the world as independent adults. They loved being independent. The more independence we gave them the more control over their lives they felt they had; there was less need for confrontation which made for a generally happy house.

Yes it was our job to care for them but I knew that the only way for them to learn something was to actually do it. As soon as they were able they did things for themselves. When they learned to brush their teeth they did it with one of us watching to make sure it was done properly. When they learned to tie their shoelaces, they did it from then on and as soon as they were able to do little jobs around the house they did them.

We made sure they knew we loved them.

We showed them how much we loved them all the time. I can remember, when I was young, the routine for waking us in the morning was the bright light in the centre of the bedroom would be turned on. There was no choice but to get up if you wanted to turn it off and at that point I was out of bed anyway. I hated it.

Because our days were so busy, morning and night time became an important time for interaction and connection with the two kids. I would creep into their room in the morning and sometimes gently ruffle their hair, give them a kiss and, while they were waking, I would open the curtains a little bit to let some light in. I talked gently to them calling them by their pet names i.e. "button" or "chicken" or, John's one for Laura, "squeaky". This was as much for my sake as theirs because if they woke up cranky and in bad humour it would make the morning more difficult, so the effort involved was worth it for everyone. Imagine how loved you would feel if someone did that for you every morning. If this is sounding a bit like the *Waltons* don't worry – there were mornings when we overslept and there was no time for any of this and it was a roar from the landing: "Lads get up – we're late. Be downstairs in 10 minutes or we'll be late for school". In general we made the effort to set our alarms so that there was plenty of time in the morning to do everything without stress and pressure and of course there was preparation the night before.

Night time was weird and wonderful – I don't really know how it evolved but at bedtime the kids used wait at the end of the stairs saying: "we're not going to bed". I would come out making monster noises and start stomping out the hallway saying "Here comes Monster Mother". They waited until the last minute and then ran screaming and scampering up the stairs and hid themselves somewhere. I spent the next few minutes going around the room stomping my feet and threatening to eat them when I found them. When I found one, usually under a bed, in the wash basket or a wardrobe, the screams and giggles echoed through the house. Now of course this wasn't a great way to get them settled for sleep, so when they had calmed down again, I left them to get ready for bed and they called one of us when they were tucked up in bed and ready for their story.

As you know, I always loved books: as a child, losing myself in stories of *The Famous Five*, *The Secret Seven*, and *Malory Towers* meant I was never bored and I was a regular visitor at the library. I really wanted the kids to develop a love of books so we read them a story every night. The easiest way to do this was to lie in our bed with a child on each side. When the kids were very young the same story suited both of them but as they got older one wanted a more grown up story so there were two stories read. Small children love hearing the same story over and over and over again. So there was a time when we read *Chicken Licken* every single night and then a time when *The Runaway Train* was on the menu. This was difficult to do I must admit, and in the end I didn't even need the book. But this is what appealed to the kids. They loved being able to say the line that was coming next and there were shrieks of: "The sky is falling down and I'm off to tell the King" night after night after night. Of course there had to be a second story then because the other child wanted something different.

Kids love fun and they love being called by pet names as it makes them feel special. I loved having fun with them – it was a chance to go back to feeling like a kid again, getting lost in the moment, playing games like hide and seek.

Technology has evolved in leaps and bounds since my kids were young. Even though they are only twenty two and twenty four the number of ways to keep kids entertained has grown rapidly in the few years since I used read bed time stories to my two. I know how tempting it is to put children in front of an X Box or some other game console and it's good to have some balance. Reading a bedtime story to your child benefits them in so many ways. It develops and re-enforces that bond between you and your child and it also helps to develop a love of learning in them. That closeness of sitting or lying together under a blanket waiting to see what is going to happen next in a story, waiting for the page to turn to see what pictures are there, and the excitement when they know what the punch line is and you both shout it out together, nothing can match it.

This is a win win situation. It's a lovely feeling lying on a bed reading a story to a child – in those few minutes you are the most important person in their world. That feeling of being able to give something magical to your child fulfils a need in you too. Parenting can be a magical experience. In giving and fulfilling a need that your child has, you receive so much in return.

The feeling of satisfaction and happiness we had when we came downstairs knowing our two precious children were upstairs asleep and happy was immense. As we made sure our children felt safe and secure I started to feel better. I was showing love, having fun, creating routines that helped for the smooth running of the house and when I sat down in the evening I had a real sense of "everything is ok in the world". *I was happy and as I made it my mission to make sure the children felt safe and secure, some of my needs were being fulfilled too. And it felt really good. I began to feel less like a passenger in my life and more like the driver. I was making decisions that were benefiting me and my family. I was regaining control over my life and how I felt and I began to feel stronger.*

What I learned:

Children need to feel safe and secure so that they can grow up healthy and happy. What you give to your kids, you get back – when you fulfil one of their needs you automatically fulfil one of your own. *In meeting your child's need for safety and security you can fulfil, among others, your need to feel that you matter and that you have a place in the world.* If you grew up feeling that you did not matter or had no important role to play, you will find that this part of you begins to heal as you step into the role of being a parent. You are the most important person in your child's life which makes this an environment that can benefit both of you.

Sometimes the road can be difficult and you will have difficult situations to deal with. What I found was that when my actions were motivated by the love I felt for my children I didn't make a mistake with them. If, and on occasions they were, my actions were motivated from anger or frustration, I regretted them. I didn't beat myself up over them but I recognised what I was doing and did my best to remember how much I loved them and let my actions come from that place. This sometimes meant making decisions that were difficult and made the kids cross i.e. as in the fire engine story, but your kids will know that you are coming from a place of love and will understand.

Your child's behaviour is driven by a need for something. The secret is finding out what that need is. A client recently told me about how her three year old child is really cranky in the mornings and whinges and moans from the moment she gets up. I asked this lady to look at her little girl and think for a moment what the child might need first thing in the morning. Straight away the mum realised that the little girl has been away from her all night and needs a little hug and a cuddle in the morning to make her feel ok. When the mum took that time, which was just a couple of minutes, in the morning, the child then happily got dressed.

I learned that what my children did and who they were are two different things. When you separate the two it is easier to stay in that feeling of love for the child and look at their behaviour more objectively. Doing my best to figure out what the child needed when they were behaving 'badly' helped me to stay in a loving space with them both.

And I learned to be present with them – leaving the work hat in the car and wearing the Mum hat when I was with them. I did my best to live in the moment with them, kiss them, cuddle them and tell them I loved them often. I still do. They might say: "Don't be soppy", but they love it. Dont' we all?

CHAPTER 9

SHAKE IT UP

One evening, when I was quite young, I was lying in bed wide awake. I had a sore lip and my mum, after applying some to my lip, had left a jar of Vaseline on the dressing table beside my bed. The walls of my bedroom were papered in lovely pink wallpaper and I remember wondering what it would be like to 'paint' the wall with the Vaseline (as you do when you are small). I sat on the bed watching in fascination as the Vaseline stain on the paper got bigger and bigger and bigger. I can remember that feeling of excitement as I scooped more and more Vaseline out of the pot and smeared it on the wallpaper watching it soak in. I knew I shouldn't be doing it but the thrill of watching that mark get bigger and bigger and bigger was just too exciting.

A bored child will find some way to make life exciting and it won't always be as harmless as what I got up to that evening.

We all need some fun and excitement in our lives. If we were to do the same thing every day we would inevitably get bored, lose interest and find it difficult to focus on what matters to us. Kids are the same. If we want them to grow up happy and healthy we have to make sure that their need for some fun and excitement is satisfied. By bringing different things into their life they stay interested and full of wonder about what else life has to offer. It's easier for them to focus when they need to if they know that they are going to do something fun at the weekend. *This need for something different in their lives is a basic need which, if we don't make sure it is met, will surely lead to them finding some other way to break the monotony and not always in a way that is beneficial to them.*

Raising our kids taught us that kids need a break from routine just as much as they need the routines themselves.

To prevent the kids from getting bored and losing interest we did our best to ensure that they had enough variety in their lives from healthy activities so that they wouldn't feel the need to engage in things that would get them into trouble. By shaking things up we started moving from a boring and monotonous way of living towards one that brought us more happiness. I started off wanting to bring some variety to my kids' routines but it turned out that we all benefitted, because we started doing things that made us all feel more alive and happy and we were doing it together. It was a win win situation for everybody.

What we did to shake it up:

We went for walks.

We created new scenarios for play and sometimes we would join in.

We got the kids to dress up.

We went swimming and cycling.

We baked.

We arranged Movie Nights.

We had their friends over.

We all let go and acted silly.

We went for walks.

When kids are bored they can get cranky and cross and start to fight. The easiest thing, weather permitting, is to put on their coats and take them out for a walk. As soon as we left the house the kids would forget what they were squabbling about and walk along picking up horse chestnuts or different types of leaves etc. Sometimes I got them to count things as we went along like how many red cars they could see? This kept them occupied as they walked and of course bred a bit of healthy competition between the two of them to see who could find the most. They always enjoyed it and the added bonus was that I felt so much better too. The fresh air and exercise helped me feel better and doing this regularly meant I was better able to cope with the normal pressure and strain of raising a family. The kids got tired from the walk and so didn't have as much energy for arguing when they got home and were happy to snuggle up on the couch with a book or play a game.

We created new scenarios for play…

One day, while visiting my mum, the two of them were getting very bored because none of their toys was there and they were just sitting listening to two adults talking. My mum took out four chairs, put a blanket over the top of them and a couple of cushions on the floor underneath and made a 'tent' for them. She handed them in a couple of pots, some spoons, some dry pasta and rice and they were suddenly transported to the 'woods' where they were camping and preparing food for themselves. This kept them occupied for ages and we were able to have our chat. It was cleaned up in two minutes before we left and they loved it so much that it became a regular thing to do in our own house when the weather was bad. It was even better at home because they had all their teddies etc. to come camping with them and tea sets etc. to make the scene even more realistic. This often kept them occupied for hours. They entered into the spirit of the whole game with gusto and each time they played it they were different characters and the story changed completely.

…and sometimes we would join in.

At times they were happy to play on their own but there were other times when I would feel a prod in my back and I would look around to be greeted by the two of them attempting to capture me and bring me to their camp where they were going to feed me all sorts of horrible concoctions. They frog-marched me into the sitting room and made me climb inside the tent where I would be told to wait while they prepared dinner. I can still remember the giggles outside the 'tent' as they put together what they said was a mixture of spiders, eye balls, creepy crawlies etc. and then they would come in and spoon feed it to me. This was great fun and I got as much entertainment out of it as they did especially when the shoe was on the other foot and I captured them. I'm sure the squeals from the pair of them, as I made up my own horrible concoctions for them to eat, could be heard down the street.

We got the kids to dress up.

When I was young we had a box of dress up clothes that my sisters and I loved to play with. The days when that box came out were absolutely great. We had long cocktail dresses that were no longer being worn and old shoes, bags and jewellery. We clip-clopped around the house pretending we were ladies of the manor and talking in really posh voices until we couldn't keep it up any more and burst out laughing. My two loved dressing up as cowboys or power rangers, Indians or scary monsters and other such characters and we had a box where we kept lots of bits and pieces for them to play with. We have some very funny photos of them that we have promised never to show anybody! They were happy for long periods of time as they changed from being one character to another and making up all sorts of stories about the lives of these people they were pretending to be. It was great fun to watch and I would often stand where they couldn't see me just to watch their antics and hear their funny voices as they entered whole-heartedly into acting out a part.

We went swimming and cycling.

Swimming was usually on a Sunday morning because it was an activity that required a couple of hours. The kids loved the water as we had brought them swimming from when they were babies. They had learned to swim when they were very young so they were very comfortable in the water. They played and swam happily in the pool for ages and were tired and hungry when they came home. We loved swimming too and because everyone was comfortable in the water we were able to relax and enjoy our swim while keeping an eye on them. It was a great activity for the whole family to take part in and it benefited all of us. It was a break from routine and a great way for us all to get some exercise.

During the summer when the kids were old enough to ride bikes we often went out in the evenings as a family, one adult in front, the two kids behind and an adult at the back. In the beginning this was a bit stressful as the kids learnt that they couldn't weave in and out on the road and there was a lot of yelling "keep in" from me as I was usually at the back watching them. However as they became more confident and consistent in cycling safely this was great fun for all of us and again helped tire the kids out. We enjoyed this time together too as it broke the monotony from the usual stuff we used to do.

We baked.

My mum taught me to bake and I wanted the kids to learn this skill too. At the weekends we regularly made pancakes for breakfast, or some queen cakes or cookies or a cake. I will admit that at the start I used let them watch because I knew there would be a mess everywhere if I let them help. However, their little faces looking longingly at what I was doing, itching to get stuck in, meant I eventually gave in and on the understanding that everyone helped with the clean-up, we all got involved. Taking it in turns, they measured, poured and mixed and then stood outside the oven peering in at their creation cooking, waiting for it to come out so they could taste it. These were some of the happiest times spent with them. I can still see the pride on their little faces as they admired their handiwork with a streak of chocolate across their mouths when they couldn't resist having a taste from the baking bowl.

And there were other days, and I can remember them well, when they simply refused to co-operate and started fighting over who was going to do what and they would be grabbing spoons off each other with shrieks of "no it's my turn". Invariably someone got hurt and ran away crying and the whole experience was ruined and I had to finish it on my own.

I was often frustrated at their behaviour because I couldn't understand it. After going to the trouble of getting out all the ingredients and utensils and taking time out from all the other things I had to do to spend this time with them, what did they go and do but ruin it all by squabbling. In the early days I used get cross about this but as time went on I realised that at those moments they weren't capable of doing anything different. *They were learning about their own feelings and figuring out for themselves how to handle them. It was going to take time for them to understand what was going on when they felt cross or frustrated and it was up to us to help them get there.*

When I questioned them after an incident like this I often found that they had agreed at some stage that it was one person's turn this time to measure and the other's to stir but that one had reneged on the agreement when they saw what was being made. This was something they had to figure out for themselves and eventually they learned to stick to what they agreed because they knew if they didn't they wouldn't get to have the fun.

Those times, when it was going well, were precious – they chatted about all the things going on in their lives as they mixed and stirred. It was a great opportunity to ask them about school, friends and anything that might be bothering them. I found that, if there was something I wanted to talk to them about or ask them, baking some biscuits or buns was a great way to get started. Because I wasn't putting them under pressure, sitting opposite them looking into their eyes and asking them the question, they were more at ease.

I remember one day when Laura was about 8 years old she came out of school very upset. Her best friend's parents were getting divorced. She was very upset about it but couldn't really say why. She said she just felt really sad. Later that evening I got out the bowls and some ingredients and we started making buns. As she sat up to the counter on a high stool mixing and measuring I started asking her about her friend. Concentrating on what was in the bowl she started to talk about how sad her friend was about her parents. She talked and talked and eventually a small voice asked "are you and Dad going to get a divorce"? This was what was playing on her mind. Her friend's parents getting divorced had rattled her little world and because it happened to her friend she felt it could happen to her too. I was able to reassure her that all was well and that this wasn't something that was going to happen. She was happy then and continued on with the baking. By speaking about what she was feeling she got the reassurance that she needed.

I found that getting the kids involved in making something with their hands meant they talked more easily. Their focus was on what they were doing and it allowed them to be less self-conscious about what they were saying. My two, like most kids, loved to talk and talk. All they needed was the opportunity in an environment where they felt at ease and baking and cooking did this for them.

Asking them to come with me for a walk and starting a chat as we walked side by side was another great way of making difficult conversations easier. Because we were walking side by side, and I wasn't looking into their faces, they felt more at ease to talk.

Varying the routine for ourselves and the kids kept us all sane. Some other things we did, and they didn't cost a lot, were movie nights, trips to the library, feeding ducks and having friends over to play.

We arranged Movie Nights.

Movie nights were great where everyone got into pyjamas, curled up on the couch under a duvet or blankets and ate popcorn while watching a movie. This was a lovely evening, often on a Friday night to celebrate the beginning of the weekend where we had more time to do things together. No one had to be up early and the kids got to stay up later than usual. They flew around the place helping out with little jobs knowing that when these were done we could all sit down and enjoy the movie. I remember when I was small how much better a movie seemed if the whole family sat down together to watch it.

Trips to the library were often on a Saturday morning or an afternoon after school. They spent a long time looking at all the books and making their choices which gave me plenty of time to browse the books of interest to me.

Feeding ducks and walks in the woods were all weekend activities that the kids looked forward to. We often gave them a choice of activities from which to choose and these were the discussions that often happened over dinner during the week. Sometimes they took it in turns to choose the activity and other times we decided. In this way everyone felt they had a voice in what we were doing as a family.

We had their friends over.

They often had friends over to the house to play and they regularly had someone stay over for the night. Of course this involved midnight feasts, giggles during the night and some shrieking as they sat up telling each other ghost stories. This brought lots of variety into their lives and it was something to look forward to at the end of a week of school and homework. It benefitted them in so many ways. They learned to compromise because their friends had lots of different ideas and in order to play together they had to let friends choose the games sometimes.

We let go and acted silly.

Having kids was an opportunity to go back and do things I always wanted to do as a child. That kid in me has always been there wanting to have fun and do mad things and so I loved playing kids' games. I allowed myself be a child again and I think this is what the kids loved. I was able to be the parent when I had to but I was able to have the fun with them too. I still love adventure and excitement and doing silly things. I love the freedom of making up stupid jokes and generally having a laugh with my two kids. Another game we played was they would say a word and I had to sing a song with that word in it. I can still remember the laughs as the silliest of songs would come to me and if I couldn't think of one I made one up. I used the time when they were small to indulge all those things that at some level I felt I didn't have enough of when I was a child. I loved watching *Winnie the Pooh* with them and was quite sad when they no longer wanted to watch it. Playing board games, splashing in the pool, playing hide and seek were all activities that I loved as much as they did.

Something I have always loved is swings. We had a swing in our back garden when I was a child and I loved to sit there going higher and higher, feeling as if I could fly and being able to see over the hedges into the neighbours' gardens for a brief second. As I grew up that love of swings stayed with me and so having kids was the perfect excuse to indulge myself and my love of swings. I had an excuse to go into playgrounds again. I loved this and when I found a playground that had swings suitable for an adult I would play away with the kids loving that feeling of going higher and higher and higher. I have often been on a swing having the time of my life and seen other mothers sitting to the side watching their kids play. I often wondered would they love to be playing too but because they were all grown up felt they couldn't? Or was I just crazy? If that is you, I say just go for it. It's great fun. We all need fun and when we just do it and don't care what others think it feels great. The child in me still gets to play and I love it. Lately I put up a swing in my garden. It has put another ghost to rest for me. I sit on that swing, going higher and higher, feeling free and happy in the knowledge that no call will come from an upstairs window to spoil the moment. I'm so grateful for the freedom I have found, for the ability to be happy and carefree and I treasure these moments hugely.

There were many advantages to all of us taking part in these activities:

It kept them occupied so they didn't get bored and start fighting with each other.

They got tired so when bedtime came they were ready to go to bed and sleep.

They were happy and there was always something to look forward to.

We all got exercise and fresh air.

As a couple it strengthened our relationship because we were doing things together.

It balanced the routine of school and homework for the kids and work and housework etc. for us.

By spending time together as a family we became very close – the kids loved spending time with us because we usually had fun.

What I learned:

Kids are capable of getting up to all sorts of mischief so do your best to stay one step ahead of them as much as you can. However, that can be exhausting so getting them out and involved in regular activities means they will be less likely to get into trouble.

Kids need some excitement in their lives. They need variety and a change from the normal routine. If we, as parents, don't provide it they will seek it out themselves and it might not always be as harmless as painting a wall with Vaseline.

As adults, we too need a change from what we do each day. As the saying goes "all work and no play makes Jack a dull boy". We look forward to the weekend when we can socialise, go to the pictures, meet up with friends, or go out to dinner. We are always looking for a break from the norm, something to do to break up the monotony and bring some interest and variety into our lives.

Adults and children need a balance between routine and variety in their lives. Kids long for the school holidays when they can have a break from routine and do something different each day. But after a while they long for the routine of school because they don't have to think about what they are going to do each day.

I can remember longing for the school holidays too when I didn't have to make lunches every morning, do the school run, oversee homework and bring them to after school activities. By the end of the summer I was longing for the routine again – to knowing what was happening each part of the day.

The secret here is balance.

We wanted to do different things with them because we had so much to show them. We wanted them to have lots of different experiences so that they could find out for themselves what they enjoyed and what made them happy. The more things they did the more likely they were to find something they really enjoyed.

I also learned that life is not meant to be taken too seriously. We are here to be happy and have fun and this can be found in the simplest of things. It's never too late to live happily ever after. Every day I choose happiness over anything else. I feel happy and grateful that I found a way out of the sadness and pain and I am determined that the rest of my life is going to be spent choosing happiness over anything else. What other people think of me is none of my business – I am content.

I want to tell you that the effort is worth it. My kids are grown up now and we still have fun. They have their lives and we have ours but we still love coming together and spending time together because the bonds that were created when they were younger are still there – the memories of the fun we had means we continue to spend time together and still have fun which creates even more memories. It's a wonderful time when they are small and it doesn't last forever so make the most of it. You will all reap the rewards.

Chapter 10

"You are unrepeatable; There is a magic about you that is all your own"- D.M. Dellinger

Kids are unique. There is no other David in the whole world the same as my David, with his auburn hair, brown eyes, warm heart, desire for independence and thirst for knowledge. There is no other Laura the same as my crazy Laura with her blonde curly hair and big blue eyes, her love of animals, cracked sense of humour and love of fun. I loved them from the moment I met them and I have fallen more in love with them with each passing day.

I had no idea who they were when they were born – all I knew was they were our kids and we had the job of looking after them as best we could. We were determined to do our best by them. We found that we spoke about them with wonder. I wonder what they will look like. I wonder what they will do when they are older. What will they like? What will they dislike? What talents will they have? What career path will they choose? These two small little human beings were entrusted to our care and it was a very important job that was ahead of us.

We are, and always have been, their biggest fans. We celebrate each milestone and sympathise with each setback. Every step of their development was greeted with enthusiasm and excitement. The grannies were called and there was genuine excitement when they first smiled or took a first step, got a first tooth, lost a tooth, used a potty, won a medal, got great marks in a test etc. We were and are constantly amazed by them. We have always been proud of them and we let them know it. They were a very important extension to the unit we created when we got married and we wanted them to know that. We were and still are a family: a group of four people who love and support each other through the ups and downs of life.

One of the things I learned about myself, when I looked back on my childhood was that I needed to feel important and that I had a place in the family. The birth of my younger sister and the subsequent abuse left me feeling displaced and it took a long time for me to find where I fitted in again.

With this knowledge I set out to make sure that my kids knew they were important, that they mattered and that they had a significant role to play in the family. *Everyone needs to feel that they are important. Feeling important, useful and appreciated makes us feel good and when we feel good we are happy and feel accepted for who we are.* When that happens we have high self-esteem and the confidence to be ourselves. That's what I wanted for David and Laura.

How we made sure that our kids felt important:

We allowed them be themselves.

We paid attention to them.

We had special time alone with each one of them.

We gave them roles.

We involved them in decisions.

We allowed them be themselves.

Firstly, if we were to rename them now, we would call them "chalk" and "cheese". They are two completely different human beings. Even though they have both grown up in the same house, they are as different from each other as two people can be. Both fabulous and both different.

When Laura was born I was so thrilled to have a girl after having a boy. I imagined shopping for pink instead of blue. Lovely girly clothes for her and there was so much choice. I imagined Laura as a real life-size doll who I could dress up. Had I a shock in store for me? In the beginning I was in control. I could dress her as I wanted. So there were pink baby grows, pink blankets, pink dresses and there was one day when the poor thing was only a few weeks old when my mum and myself pulled a pair of tiny white tights over her scrawny little legs, popped a pink and white dress and a little white cardigan on her and sat back and admired her. Well I'm glad we had that bit of fun because as soon as Laura found her voice it was a different story altogether.

"I hate girls' clothes" were some of her earliest words "and my curls". One day I found her in the kitchen with a safety scissors in her hand. She was chopping away at her hair and managing to cut off her beautiful blonde curls. She was a tomboy. She did not want to wear any clothes unless they came from the boys' section of a shop. And so, even though I was disappointed that I couldn't buy the lovely things I had imagined, that's what I bought her. My mum, who always had us turned out as if we were about to meet the Queen when we were small, was shocked. She could not understand why I did not put my foot down and insist that Laura wear clothes that I chose for her. But my little girl was happy – climbing trees, on skateboards, bikes, and roller blades, all the time dressed similarly to David. They were regularly mistaken for brothers especially when Laura was very young and her hair was short. This made her very happy indeed and she often came running in with a big smile on her face, saying someone thought she was a boy. We couldn't say "You're the best girl", we had to say "you're the best boy" to her.

Laura was a tomboy. How could I object? I had turned into quite a tomboy myself and loved nothing better than to play with my brother and his friends once I left the dolls behind. It was much better fun playing cops and robbers. Even though I was disappointed that I couldn't buy the lovely clothes I wanted to for her, I knew that it really wasn't important. I was glad that she was happy to wear clothes as I knew of one mother whose child refused to wear clothes at all. Now that was a difficult one. I accepted her for who she was. Instead of fretting about it, we celebrated it and bought her cool boys clothes and she thrived.

When David was young all his friends were playing rugby, soccer or hurling. We went along with David to each of these a couple of times but he absolutely hated the games. Instead, as both of us were musicians, we sent him for piano lessons and he loved it. He also loved drama and so for several years he attended stage school and music lessons. He had found what he loved. Of course he also loved gathering ingredients from the kitchen and mixing them in jars in the garden shed to find out what would happen. Despite the stink that often emanated from the bottom of the garden we indulged this interest, jokingly calling him "the mad scientist". He had a lot of different interests and we encouraged him in whatever he got excited about. Today he has finished his degree in Industrial Biochemistry and is working as a Lab Analyst, speaks Spanish, German and Polish and is a great musician. I look back and think about how differently things would have turned out if we had insisted he keep attending soccer, rugby or hurling "because that's what boys do". By us being open and attentive to the uniqueness of our children, it allowed them to grow into the human beings they were destined to be.

Sometimes we can be afraid of what people will think, i.e. "your son doesn't play sport?" Horror!, or "your daughter wants to dress like a boy"? Weird!

We found that loving and celebrating our children for the people they were helped them to feel safe, secure and confident of their place in the world. Today, they have lots of self-confidence, high self-esteem and a self-belief that is inspiring.

We paid attention to them.

Did you ever walk into a room full of people and no one turned to you to say hello?

Have you ever come home and everyone is watching television and it's not even muted for a second to say "hi"?

How did you feel?

When David or Laura came home from anywhere I made sure that I stopped what I was doing and went to them to give them a hug and say "hi". I would ruffle their hair or give them a kiss and in this way they knew they were missed and someone was glad to see them back. I liked to let them know I was glad they were there and that I was happy to see them. They were a significant part of my life and this was a simple way of letting them know it.

We had special time alone with each one of them.

Let me share a story told to me by a lady recently. She grew up in a house with three older sisters and there was a gap of seven years between her and the next youngest girl. There were also two boys younger than her. As you can imagine this was a very busy house. One Christmas Eve this girl's mum caught her by the hand and said: "come on, you and me, let's go down to see the crib in the church". The girl was only six at the time but to this day that Christmas sticks out in her mind as being the best Christmas of her life. She had time with her mum all by herself. She told me that she and her mum had skipped down the road to the church and she felt so special for that time that it stayed with her forever. I think we sometimes forget how easy it is to give our children what they need. This girl's eyes got teary as she remembered that Christmas Eve as she had never forgotten that feeling of being singled out for a special treat.

You can arrange to spend some time alone with each of your children. It doesn't have to be expensive or for very long. Going to a coffee shop for a cup of tea and a bun or going for a walk just the two of you – anything at all that makes the child feel special. It might seem simple to you but to the child it can mean a lot. I think that is something that happens as we get older. We can think we need more and we think our kids are the same. Please keep reminding yourself that your kids' needs are simple. It doesn't take a lot of effort and the effort you do make has a big impact on your child. My kids still remember spending time with me without the other kid in tow; a special time where they didn't have to compete with the other to be heard; when they had my full attention and we just had a pleasant time. Often it was just a walk to the shop hand in hand for an ice-cream.

Treasure the time when they are young as, before you know it, they will be all grown up. So, spend time with them, get to know them, love them, hug them, chat with them, listen to them and play with them.

We gave them roles.

Give them responsibility for some jobs around the house. Let them know that their presence matters enormously. They might not like the jobs you give them to do but it contributes hugely to their sense of belonging. David and Laura had lots of little jobs. One was emptying the dishwasher. Laura was responsible for the lower tray and David for the top tray. This was simply because one was taller and could reach the higher presses. When they couldn't reach something they simply left it on the worktop for me to put away but they still had to empty it. This was their responsibility and they knew that if they didn't do it then there was no place to put the dirty dishes and this would upset how the kitchen got cleaned up after dinner. Their role was an important one.

When the kids were young we often went to the Saturday market. Sometimes as a treat we would go to a café for breakfast. The café was self-service. Often we arrived at the table and the kids wanted ketchup or butter that they had forgotten. Rather than us getting up and getting it for them we encouraged them to go and ask a waiter for it. We could see them all the time so we knew they were safe and they learnt to be able to ask for what they wanted from a very young age. In the beginning they were a bit shy but we encouraged them to go and get it. The more they did this the more their confidence grew and after a while they were jumping up and down wanting to go and get something. We wanted to create a feeling in the children that they have value, are useful and are able to do things for themselves.

I know as you read this you might be thinking: "It's easier to just get up and get it myself – I'm faster" but, as the ultimate goal is raising independent adults, don't forget that saying "Rome wasn't built in a day". Children do not just happen to become independent adults overnight at a certain age. It's all the little things over time that create the adults they will become.

We needed to have patience when they made mistakes or when it took a little longer to get something done or when it wasn't done as well as we could have done it ourselves.

In the case of the café: are you able to walk?, are you able to talk? – right then you are able to get your butter.

Of course the up side of this was we were able to sit back and enjoy our coffee while they looked after themselves. Win win!

We involved them in decisions.

Involving the children in the jobs that needed to be done around the house, in deciding how we spent a free day, what we had for dinner sometimes, what movie to watch on television, all contributed to instilling a sense of value and self -worth in them. The temptation was to be in control of everything that happened but that could have then contributed to them finding negative ways of getting that feeling of "I'm somebody".

Do you remember how I said that I felt that the abuse had, in some way, contributed to giving me a feeling of importance? I understood that this need was still there. We all need to feel that we matter: that we have a place in this world and that we are important. As I ensured that my children's need to feel valued was met, I became aware of how important the role I was playing in their lives was. As I worked to mother them in my own unique way, I realised my need to feel I mattered was being met. I had found my place again, a significant role as their mother, and another little piece of me began to heal.

What I learned:

Kids are perfect diamonds. When they are born they are absolutely perfect in every way. They are born exactly as they are meant to be. This takes a lot of pressure off us as parents. We don't have to change them or make them into something. I learned that my job as a parent was not to mould them into what I thought they should be or what society thought they should be but rather help them discover who they are. Our kids are unique individuals with specific talents and a specific role to play in this world of ours. If we had insisted on trying to mould them into something else, I know they would not have been happy. However if we really get to know them, by observing them and listening to them, and allow them to discover things for themselves they will find out for themselves who they really are.

Treating them as important human beings gave them a sense of belonging in this world. This was done in small ways when they were little like getting them to help with the washing up, asking their opinion and allowing them the freedom to dress as they chose.

Ignoring other people's opinions and really trusting what I felt was the right thing to do really helped me be the best mum to the kids. I listened to my heart and if a choice I was making felt right inside, then I went with it. On the other hand, if a choice I was making felt as if I was making it because I was afraid of what others would think or say, then I would think more about it and do my best to make the choice that was right for the children.

I also learned that when we make the effort to make decisions based on what our heart is telling us, those decisions are never wrong. I found that when I treated the kids this way we developed a fantastic relationship that has grown stronger as time goes by.

For myself, the need I had as a child and still have, to feel that I matter, was more than fulfilled as I made decisions based on my heart. I became a very significant person in their lives with a very important role to play to help the two of them discover who they were. I gained as much, if not more, than they did through the process.

CHAPTER 11

WHAT'S LOVE GOT TO DO WITH IT?

What is love? When it comes to our children what does it mean? Well I googled it to see what would come up, and I came across this quotation, which I really liked:

"Try to see your child as a seed that came in a packet without a label. Your job is to provide the right environment and nutrients and to pull the weeds. You can't decide what kind of flower you'll get or in which season it will bloom" – Anonymous.

Unconditional love isn't just about what we feel towards our children. It's more about what they feel. It means they don't have to be or do anything in particular to earn our love. We love them exactly as they are. Love is the absence of judgement.

We can often let fear get in the way of loving our kids. Fear of how they will turn out. Fear of whether or not you are doing things right. Fear of what other people will think. When will he walk? She's taking forever to learn to talk. Why does he keep fighting with his sister? Why does she constantly answer back? Fear of whether or not your kids will love you. Fear of being alone. So many fears leave no room for love. ***Get out of your head. Stop thinking. Start feeling.*** Start feeling that love you have for your child and your actions will be guided effortlessly and easily. When you love someone, you want the best for them without looking for something in return. That is real love. Your actions will always be right when they are guided by that love. You will want to spend time with them. You will want to play with them, listen to them and read to them. You will want to share stories of when you were small because you know they will be interested to hear what life was like back then; when there was no electricity and dinosaurs as my kids used to think. You will remember the names of their stuffed animals because you know that means a lot to them. You will put a note in their lunch box saying "I love you" because you know that will make them smile to themselves and feel loved and cherished even if they scoff at it in front of their friends. You will ask them for help because you know what it feels like to feel needed. Even if it's easier to do the job yourself, you will still ask because you want your child to feel needed and special. You will ask their opinion on where to go for a day out because you know what it's like to have your opinion valued. You will make their birthday special because you know what you feel like on your birthday. I still feel a bit like a kid on my birthday. I want it to be special. It's my day. I want to be spoilt. It is a special day. The one day in the year that is especially for me. So you make that day special for your child – you make an extra effort to make sure they feel extra special that day.

When you are in the flow of really loving your kids, you remember that when they are misbehaving they are still your kids and you love them. You know they are not the behaviour they are carrying out. If they are behaving badly, you recognise there is a reason for it. You make the effort to find out why they are behaving that way instead of getting hung up on what they are doing. You let them know that you love them anyway but that the behaviour is not ok.

Maybe the reason he is acting up is because he feels you love his sister more and he has lost that special relationship with you since the baby arrived.

Maybe the reason she is arguing so much is that she thinks you don't really understand what she is trying to say.

Remember it is just fear that is getting in the way of you really letting go and loving your child. When you can let that fear go and get into the essence of who you are, you will find that the love flows easily. You will find yourself drawn to doing things you never thought you would.

You will stop being distracted by the phone, laptop, iPad, etc. when they are around. You will praise them for their achievements. You will chat with them about what they can improve. Your praise will be genuine and given where it is deserved. You won't be inclined to just praise everything they do because they will know that you don't mean it. You won't be afraid to ask them if they could have done better and, if so, how you can help them achieve that.

You will understand who they are: the tomboy, the musician, the sports person, the creative one, the one who loves maths, the one who is afraid of the dark or of spiders. You will take the time to know them: who they really are. You will let them know that they are number one in your life.

When you are in the flow of really loving your child, you will apologise to them if you make a mistake that has hurt them. You will be polite to them and not hurt them or use abusive language to them. You will keep your promises to them because you know how bad you feel if someone breaks a promise to you. You will keep their little secrets. You will reward their achievements with a special meal or book or something that lets them know you have seen them make an effort and that it paid off.

Please dump the fear. I was so afraid in the beginning. I was so afraid that I would do things wrong. When I got rid of the fear and allowed myself to really feel the love I felt for my two gorgeous kids I knew things would work out ok.

Get out of your head and into your heart. That's the secret. The secret to being the best parent you can be. Forget about the neighbours, the friends, family etc. and what they will think. Remember everyone is conditioned by their own upbringing as to what is right and wrong with regard to raising kids. When you are acting from your heart you will not make a mistake. You will be coming from a place of love instead of fear.

The reward for yourself when you come from that place as a parent is immense. You feel really good too. This is your natural state and it feels good to go there. This is what people are searching for. People are always searching for love – look at the number of songs that are written about it. And yet we keep getting stuck in fear. Mainly fear that we won't be able to handle it if people criticise our way of parenting. And people probably will regardless of what you do. My mum didn't approve of the way I allowed Laura dress. But that was coming from fear. She was afraid of what people would think if they saw Laura dressed in boy's clothes. I just looked at Laura and saw the happiest kid in the world.

The secret is love. It's the key to making parenting easy. We get caught up in our stories about what being a good parent means. We fret over how we will discipline our kids, how much telly they should watch, how much study they should be doing, how many extra-curricular activities should they be involved in, how do they compare with our friends' children, how much pocket money should they have, am I spoiling them and what will become of them if they don't want to go to college and so on and so on. The list of things we can worry about is endless. Sometimes we can be so programmed to worry that when we don't have something to worry about we worry that we're not caring enough and we worry about that.

The common denominator for all these questions that swirl around in our head is fear. Fear about whether or not we are doing a good job at this parenting thing. "Am I good enough?" is a common question that comes into our minds. Everywhere we look we are bombarded with advertisements telling us what we should be doing to ensure we are being a good parent and we are often afraid to trust our own decisions, and so we allow others to add to the fear we are already feeling about not being good enough. We start to believe that we need to buy our kids things, feed them certain things and let them go certain places in order to make us a good parent.

Kids don't come with a "user manual" and we feel as if we don't have a clue what we are doing and so we read all the books and listen to all the words of advice and begin to believe that everyone else knows better than us because they have done it before and we haven't.

Trust yourself and you will no longer feel afraid. *Having kids is a natural process and so is nurturing them. Everything you need is there waiting for when you need it.* It's not something out there that you need to learn. Does a dog need to learn how to take care of its puppies? Trust your intuition. Advice comes thick and fast from all sorts of places, so listen and decide for yourself what is right or wrong for your family.

Maybe you haven't had a perfect childhood. Maybe you have never experienced unconditional love and feel afraid that you will be useless at this because you have nothing but bad stuff to use as a reference. That is perfectly understandable and what I have noticed is that people who have had unpleasant experiences in their childhood seem even more determined to create something different for their kids. If that is what you want, then it takes commitment to create that better life for them. It won't happen automatically, so you have to step up and decide that you want it for them, and be willing to do what it takes to get it.

Most of us were products of parents who didn't fully understand the importance of letting us know we were perfect human beings just as we were. Most of us didn't experience unconditional love because our parents were products of their time and the awareness of how important this is just wasn't there. Some people had horrible childhoods. If yours were less than perfect parents, as we all are, look back at what was going on for your parents and see if you can understand, even a little, why they behaved as they did. What need in themselves were they trying to meet when they behaved as they did? *Finding it in your heart to feel some compassion for them and their story will start you on a journey to forgiving them which will ultimately make you feel better.* Finding a way to forgive is the greatest gift you can give yourself. Forgiveness is about you not them. It's not about saying what happened or the way you were brought up was ok if it wasn't. It is about freeing yourself from the pain of the past so that you embrace where you are now and be the kind of parent you want to be. Keep searching until you can find a way to understand your parents and find some compassion in your heart for them. If you keep looking you will find it.

Could you, just for a minute, consider thinking about it differently? How could this experience have benefitted you? Yes, benefitted you. What can you learn from the experience that you can use now with your children? How did you feel? Do you want something different for your children? How might that experience help you become a better parent? You will find that as you do this the old negative feelings you thought you would have to live with forever will gradually fall away and you will become happier. You can embrace the past as a place where you learned what you needed to in order to prepare you for this journey as a parent. Reflect on your childhood regularly so that you can avoid making the mistakes your parents did. Remember each generation makes its own set of mistakes. You will make yours and your children may be critical in the future of some things you did, so be gentle on yourself.

Love yourself by forgiving yourself for holding on to this pain. It's possible that you have held on to the pain of your childhood for a very long time. Maybe you never felt you mattered or were good enough. Maybe you were starved of affection. Maybe you felt that no one cared. Perhaps these feelings have been with you for as long as you can remember and they may have influenced every relationship you ever had. Maybe you are frightened that your kids will feel the same as you did. These are all very real fears that I have heard people express. You didn't know you could let all those feeling go and move forward but you can.

Maybe you had a fantastic childhood and grew up feeling loved and cherished but aren't sure that you will be able to do the same for your children. Maybe you are afraid that you have become too selfish. Whatever your story is, remember it is just that, a story. It's the stuff you keep telling yourself in your head and it's not necessarily true.

Learning to forgive yourself is a very valuable tool that you will need throughout the years of parenting your child. *Despite your best efforts there will be days when you lose your cool and you shout or say things in anger. There will be days when you are too tired to play with them or give them what they need. This isn't about being perfect. It's about doing your best day to day.* Say sorry and move on. When you say sorry to your kids you are telling them that it is ok to make mistakes if you really are sorry afterwards. This gives them permission to be less than perfect too.

This chapter is all about letting go of fear and switching over to a feeling of love. When your actions come from a place of love they will be exactly what you and your children need in that moment in time. That moment is all you have. It's not about yesterday or tomorrow, it's about today and this moment you have with them. Are you feeling love for them or are you caught up in some story you are telling yourself about them, like they should be brighter, livelier, happier, faster?

I thought love was a feeling. I thought it was that feeling I had for my family, friends and husband. I thought it was how I felt when I was with them. I thought it was something that could be taken away and I would be left without it. Like most people I thought it was something I needed to get from someone else. So I looked to my husband and was eager to have children to help me experience that unconditional love that people sing about and write about. What I discovered was something that surprised and amazed me and was incredibly simple.

Love isn't out there! *Love isn't something you get from someone else. It can't be taken away. It's you – the source of love is you.* It begins with each one of us. It's who we are – our natural state. Everything else is something we have learned over time. We have learned to be afraid.

Love is not something that can be given to us. *And if it can't be given to us, it can't be taken away.* Love isn't something that is out there. You are the source of love. Love comes from you. You have a choice in every moment to feel love or to not feel love.

When I was thinking about having children I thought about how much I would love them, how I would care for them, encourage them, teach them and make their childhood happy. I never really thought about what I would get in return except I knew that I would be happy doing this. I expected that they would love me in return but my lessons in love went a lot deeper over the years. In the early days I think I was looking for something from them. I was looking outside myself for love. If I give them this, then I'll get that from them. I thought love meant making sure they were properly nourished, had clean clothes, were hugged and kissed and told they were loved, were played with and given the best education we could give them. I thought it meant teaching them things and exposing them to lots of extra-curricular activities. I thought it was about all the things that come to mind when we think about raising happy and healthy kids. Yes, these are all different ways of showing that we care about them but real love is a lot simpler.

When we allow love to flow from us in each and every moment we experience real love. Yes each and every moment. What does that mean? It's easy to love kids when they are behaving 'well'. It's easy to love them when they are being 'good'. It's easy to love them when they get good results at school. It's easy to love them when they are being helpful around the house and speaking nicely to you. It's easy to love them when they are behaving the way you want them to and when they follow the path you think they should. Yes, when they are doing what we think they should and turning out to be the people we want them to be, it's easy to feel love.

What about the times when they are being 'difficult'? The times when they are cranky, cross, disagreeable, opinionated and determined to do the opposite of what you think they should? What about the times they are throwing a tantrum in the middle of the supermarket? When they are afraid and not as strong as you think they should be? What about the times when they can't be bothered to do homework or work at school? The times when they say "in a while" to you asking them to do something? The times when they leave a mess around the house and you are tearing your hair out in frustration? What about if they get pregnant when they are just seventeen years old? What about if they told you they are lesbian or gay? What about if they didn't get the job or career you thought they should? What then? Do we withhold love from them until they row in and do what we want them to and be the people we expected them to be?

What we discovered, and we experienced a lot of the above situations, is that this is when you find out what real love is.

The way to experience real love is to give love. If we keep waiting for love to come from someone else we will be waiting a long time. *By loving what there is in each and every moment you experience love.* This is true of all your relationships but here we are focusing on kids. When you accept your children for the human beings they are, you will experience love. When you are kind to them you will experience love. When you are open to whatever comes your way with them you experience love. When you don't want to change a single hair on their heads you experience love. It's by loving them that the love flows back to you. You benefit as much from loving your children as they do because, as your heart opens to loving them exactly as they are, you experience love. That feeling you have been searching for. When it is returned, it is real love you get back; not just love because you are their mum or dad but real love for who you are. Love is a way of being, not something we get from someone else. The love we get from other people is a bonus.

So what can get in the way of us having this loving feeling for our kids? The answer is fear. What will people think? If I don't insist on them being a particular way, how will they turn out? Will they get a good job? What will become of him or her? What will the neighbours think? What will my friends say? Will they think I'm a bad mother or father? What will people think of me? The competition between parents starts when kids are very young. I spoke with a mother recently who told me how her friend is constantly on the phone to her telling her about her young son; how many words he can say, how many steps he can take, how clever he is and how she has his whole life mapped out for him but also wants to know how this lady's child is doing so that she can compare.

Are we using our children as a way of making ourselves look and feel good? Are we using our children? Do we need them to be a particular way in order for us to be happy? Do we need them to get good results, be pretty and successful for us to love them?

I was recently in a clothes shop and overheard a mum of a young girl, about thirteen or fourteen years of age, tell her daughter that if the size 8 didn't fit she would have to go on a diet. What does it say about us if our daughters don't have 'the perfect figure'? How does it reflect on us if our child isn't the 'A' student? What does it mean about our parenting if our child makes a mistake and become pregnant at 17? What will people think of us? Do we need our kids to make ourselves look good?

Are we really loving our children? My child is doing really well at school so I must be a good parent. My child is really pretty: look at what we created. My child has such good manners, can play the piano so well, is so advanced in his or her reading, all the teachers love her etc. etc… "Oh I love her so much."

If you are looking for reasons why you love your child you are missing out on the greatest feeling in the world: real love that comes from loving them for who they are. Loving and accepting them for the beautiful people they are whether they do well at school or not. Whether they learn to talk and walk at 4 instead of 2 years of age. Whether they dance like an elephant or ballerina. Whether or not they have a note in their heads or can sing like Pavarotti. Choosing love in every moment allows you to experience peace, joy and contentment. There is no place for fear when we choose love.

We always have a choice. We can choose to go the route we have been programmed to go on or we can drop down into love. We have been conditioned to make judgements about everybody and we often voice these judgements when they are better left unsaid. Love is the absence of judgement. When you really love your kids you don't judge them. Remember your opinion of what is right and wrong is based on your own upbringing and conditioning. Sometimes, and I do this very often, we have to stop and ask if what we are thinking is actually serving us now in this moment. Is it creating a feeling of peace and joy in your home or is it causing stress and upset and fear? If you don't like how you are feeling, you have the choice to change. You can choose love now. Choose to feel love for your child instead of being afraid.

When you choose love instead of fear, your words and actions will evoke a completely different response from your kids. They will feel the love and respond with love to you.

It's a conscious choice you make in each and every moment of each and every day. Some days it will be easy and other days it will be very difficult. You will feel anger and sadness, frustration and apathy. As you begin to choose love you will become conscious of when you are choosing something else instead. You will begin to recognise that it is a choice. It's not something that is happening to you. In each and every moment that you choose love you will see how you feel better and the response from those around you is different. *Love is the most powerful energy there is.* I have found that it can turn situations in my life around 360 degrees when I need it to.

Love is for giving, not for getting. When we give love to others it fills us with peace, joy, happiness and kindness. We feel compassion for others and we have lots of patience. When we interact with our children filled with those feelings, it allows them to relax and be happy and content too. Choosing love will be the best choice you ever make. It's choosing love over that little voice in your head that says "you should be angry here", "you should do something", "they need to be punished", "they did something wrong", "stick up for what is right".

You will know you have chosen the path of love because it feels right when you do. When you have gone with that voice in your head, the voice of fear, it feels horrible. You feel upset or angry and you feel separate from your children.

When you choose love you listen to them and try to understand what is going on for them when they misbehave. When they are upset you sit and ask them what is wrong rather than telling them to "grow up" or "that's no reason to be upset". When you choose love you feel good. When you choose love you teach your children a completely different way of handling conflict. It teaches them to open their hearts and to be compassionate to others too. This creates a deep sense of happiness and contentment in your children which is what we hear a lot of people saying about their kids: "I just want them to be happy". We all know how good it feels to be happy. However we often think that we need something to make us feel that way. We forget that we have the choice here and now to be happy if we choose to feel love for life exactly as it is in this moment. In a split second that happiness can disappear and that is because you are no longer feeling love but have gone back in to confusion and fear. Finding just a tiny bit of love for the here and now can be exactly what you need to take you back in to that feeling of happiness and peace.

This all takes some effort. It's not difficult but it is about making a conscious decision to feel love in this moment. You have to want something different. Sometimes it can be just that we have enough of the fear and the worry that brings us on this journey to choosing love. For me I chose to look beyond the behaviours I didn't like, the tantrums, the fighting that went on between the two of them, the times they were selfish or uncaring. I made the choice to love them regardless. I always wanted this sense of love with my kids. I wanted to love them, I wanted them to feel love and so that is what I chose. That's how I learnt the power of love.

Who made you God? That is a question I often asked myself when I found myself making a judgement about what was right and what was wrong about what the kids were doing. Who am I to say that my kids should be this or that? Who am I to say they should get a certain number of points in their exams? Who am I to say they should go to college? Who am I to say they should be anything? Yes, we had our opinions on what was right and wrong, and we guided them accordingly because that was part of our role. But who am I to say when they should or should not be upset, what career they should choose, how much effort they should put in to something. How can I know what is true for each of them? *My beliefs about what they should or should not be doing are based on just that – my beliefs. By loving them as they are I allow them to make their own choices.* This doesn't mean not teaching them right and wrong but it's about listening to them and really hearing what it is that they want and supporting them in that. It's about making suggestions, opening their minds to different possibilities. It's about exploring options with them, opening their eyes to what life can be like for them. That was what love meant for me. When kids feel heard they are more open to your advice but if they feel you are dictating to them they can be more inclined to switch off and hear nothing you have to say. When you really love them they can feel it. They may not make the choices you would like but you love them anyway. By doing this not only do they feel good but you feel good too. There is no worry or fear or fretting or anxiety. Just love. You trust they will have the experiences they need to make them strong, healthy and happy human beings.

When you come from a place of love with your kids you are predictable. Your kids know where they stand with you. They know you will accept them and love them regardless of what they do with their lives. If they fail an exam, if they lose their school jumper or books, if they tell you a lie, if they are angry and upset, if they are rude, if they do the exact opposite of what you wanted them to do you love them anyway. You may not like the behaviour but they know you love them. They are just little human beings learning and growing just like you did. The greatest gift we can give them is love for exactly who they are in any moment, be that a little bundle of happiness and giggles or a ball of anger and hate. These are just emotions and behind all that there is your little child just wanting to be loved. When you love your child you are teaching them to love and love will flow from and to them and when this happens they feel joy, peace, happiness and contentment and so do you.

Switch your awareness to this very moment and find something to love about it. Now do it again and again. Every time you think about it find something to love. This is how you start. The next time your child does something where your normal reaction would be to get cross, find something to love. Notice how good that feels. Notice how they are behaving in that moment. Notice how you still love that little child but their behaviour is making you cross. Look at their little cheeks, those little eyes looking up at you. Focus on how much you love them and notice how you respond differently. You will probably find you are curious as to why they behaved that way. What was it they needed in that moment that caused them to behave that way? Were they feeling a bit insecure, were they bored or are they just finding a way to get your attention because they need a little love, a little hug, a kind word or some time with you when you are not busy. When you notice what it is and you give it to them you will feel really good and so will they.

Your child needs to know that you love them through all the emotional ups and down that they experience. When your child is throwing a tantrum in the supermarket they need to know that you love them anyway. They are feeling out of control with all the emotions they are experiencing and they need you to tell them they are still loved and that things are ok.

The more you do this the more your confidence as a parent will grow. You will see how well this works and how peaceful and happy a home you can have. There will be no need for the raised voices, your kids will be happy and content and so will you. You will feel really empowered and in control because you will realise that you have the power to choose love in each and every moment. *Don't worry if you don't do it all the time. Each time you don't you will notice how different and unpleasant it feels and you will be more determined to choose love the next time the need arises.* What a wonderful gift this will be to you and your children. Your children will grow up using love as a way of solving conflicts rather than anger. This will bring more peace and contentment to them too.

When you are coming from a place of love with your children you will be totally present with them. When you are reading a story to them you are thinking of that moment only, enjoying the sensation of being cuddled up with them, watching their little faces as they eagerly wait for the bit of the story they know when they can shout out the recurring sentence, e.g. in *Chicken Licken* "the sky is falling down and we're off to tell the King". You will be in the moment just reading the story and enjoying this precious time with them. You will not be thinking "how fast can I get this read so that I can get downstairs and get the kitchen tidied and the washing in the machine so I can put my feet up"?

Be fully present with them. Do you remember when they were born? Do you remember that beautiful smell from the top of their head? Do you remember that lovely feeling of just being with them? Do you remember holding them in your arms as you examined their tiny fingers and toes? They didn't have to do anything. They were perfect just as they were. Has that changed and, if so, what happened?

This exercise is about becoming conscious again to these wonderful human beings. We can help ourselves to become really present to them through our senses.

Firstly look at them. Observe them as they chat to you. Really look at them. Look at their face, their hands and their hair. Take the time to really look at them and notice everything about them. Without judgement about what is good or bad or nice or not; just observe.

Next listen to them – listen to the sound of their voice. Listen to what they are saying. Listen to how their voice rises and falls depending on how excited they are about something.

Next, feel your heartbeat and theirs. Feel their little arms around your neck. Feel the softness of their skin. Feel the heat or cold in the room. Feel their breath on your skin.

Now feel that love and warmth you have for them. Feel that nurturing side of you. Feel how powerful you are and the safety and security you are providing for them.

Now taste the air around the two of you. Taste their skin as you plant a kiss on their cheek.

And now smell that unique scent that is your child; the smell of the outdoors if they have been playing outside or the fresh smell after they have had a lovely warm bath.

Now start again and use all your senses to take it all in. This is how you can start to become really present with your child.

Next you will notice how everything intensifies. Colours will seem brighter and you will begin to see your child as they truly are. You will stop having pre-conceived ideas about who they are and who they will become. Now this is love. *It is a state of being not a feeling.*

"Where did the time go?" I hear so many parents say. One minute they were small and the next thing they're leaving home. We can only do one thing at a time – many people think they can multi-task, but in reality, if we are to do something wholeheartedly, it has to be one thing at a time. So much of our time we spend in the past, wishing we could change it or in the future hoping we can influence it. The fact is that no matter how hard we try we cannot change the past, it's written in stone and we can only change how we relate to it and how it affects us now. We can help to influence the future but really things have a way of just happening the way they are supposed to, so it's not worth spending too much time there either. The best way to influence the future is by being present to each moment and doing our best there, but what we usually do is just use the present moment as a stepping stone to somewhere else. That's why we often have the feeling that life is passing us by. We are creating that feeling ourselves by not being present to the moment.

The next time you are playing with your child, use all your senses to be fully present. If you are giving them a bath, feel the water in your hand. Feel the bubbles as you wash their hair. Listen to their chatter as they play with their bath toys. Notice the scent of the shampoo. Be there instead of being in your head thinking about other things. It will be a lovely experience for you and your child.

Our brains are so used to being active and thinking about one thing after the other. *We can learn to stop that endless chatter and become present.* A quick technique to help you to be present is using your breath. When emotions are high, pause for a second and take some deep breaths. Breathe in deeply and then out through your nose. As you breathe out put a smile on your face. It's impossible to feel angry with a Cheshire grin on your face. Your body relaxes and you can see the moment for what it is. If it's that your child has just dropped his plate of dinner on the dog we can see it for what it is; your child developing his motor skills and making an error, nothing more. If your child has thrown his dinner at the dog, it's simply your child trying to come to understand his own emotions. It's not a deliberate attempt to ruin your day. As you breathe, you can imagine that you are breathing in loving energy and as you breathe out, you can imagine that all the negative emotions are leaving your body. Teach this technique to your children and you will be giving them a gift for life; an effective, simple tool to take charge of their own emotional state. The best way to teach is by example and when they see Mum and Dad doing this to take control of their emotions, they will want to copy and do the same. What a peaceful, compassionate and joyful home you can create.

Your children are constantly giving you opportunities to become present with them. Every time they admire some lovely flowers, or the clouds or a little kitten. Every time they pull at your hand to stop and examine something. How many times have we grabbed them by the hand, urging them to hurry so we can be somewhere else? Being present with your child helps you to see life from their perspective and every time you do this the bond between you will grow and with this comes trust. They will know you 'get them'. They will trust that you will see things from their point of view and will seek you out for advice and help with solving their little problems.

In everyday life being present with your kids could mean simply turning off the radio when you are in the car and listening and chatting with them about their day. Really listening, in a non-judgemental way, and asking appropriate questions, helps them know that you are paying attention and not thinking about dinner or bills. Connecting with them in this way lets them know that they are more important than that email, that book you are reading, the television, radio or Facebook. They then learn to trust you and when they trust you it is you they will turn to when they need help. They will know how important they are to you and they will know you are ready and willing to stop what you are doing to be there for them. They won't have to compete with your work or all the different things that pull us away from being totally with them. *Kids know when you are not present with them. They can sense it. And they will often just become quiet because they know you are not paying attention.* How many times have you realised that your child has been talking to you but you have no idea what they said? You might see them shrug their shoulders and when you ask them to repeat they respond with "oh it's nothing".

A great mantra that I used use was "this too will pass". It helped me stay calm when there was fighting or tantrums. I knew this time would end and that everything would be calm again. And remember these beautiful days that you have with your children will end and they will grow up and they won't need you to read them a story or kiss a scraped knee. They won't need you to teach them or hug them or listen to them. They will grow up into independent adults just like you did and they won't need you anymore. These are valuable and precious times. Tell them you love them every day. Hug them and kiss them. Let them know you love them unconditionally. They don't have to be anything or do anything. Let them know you love them no matter what. You may not see immediate results but you will look back and be so happy that you made the effort. Children are a precious gift. They have been entrusted to you so that you can teach them and also so that you can learn from them. They can have a huge part to play in healing your own wounds if you commit to wanting something better for them.

When your heart fills with love there is no room for anger, sadness, fear, hurt or guilt. What you focus on gets bigger. If you focus on love that is what you will experience. By filling my heart with love for these two precious children, really focusing on it and feeling it, all the old horrible feelings I had got pushed out. It was really exciting to watch this happen in myself; the more love I felt, the more reasons to feel love there were.

What I learned:

Kids are a blessing given to some and not to others. They are entrusted to us to love and to care for. It's our job to help them grow and evolve as they are meant to; not as we want them to. Yes, it is our duty to make sure they learn how to behave in society, we teach them manners, we educate them, we love them and we allow them to grow as nature has intended them to. It is not up to us to mould them into what we think they should be according to our standards. It is up to us to encourage them to find out who they are, what makes them happy, why they are here and who they are destined to become.

If we get in the way of this by projecting our own fears and inadequacies onto them we are getting in the way of them fulfilling their full potential.

From the beginning, we gave the kids the freedom to express themselves – they had opinions and those opinions were important. We listened, not always agreeing, but listened and let them know that their opinion counted.

Finally, I learned that a heart filled with love has no choice but to heal.

Chapter 12

"Be Yourself – Everyone else is already taken" - Oscar Wilde

It's taken me a long time to be fully comfortable with who I am. I felt ashamed of what had happened to me and afraid that people would think differently about me if they knew the truth. I didn't want people to feel sorry for me. From when I was a child I have often felt obliged to do things and be someone I didn't want to be. I was afraid to do anything different. I was conditioned from a young age to act in certain ways in order to feel loved and accepted. Everybody wants to feel loved, but we are sometimes afraid that if people see the true version of us that they will walk away. This is where I first lost my sense of who I am, pretending to be someone else for a long time: a person stronger than I was with a childhood like I thought everyone else had experienced.

I built a wall around me to protect myself from being hurt any more. I was safe in there. But it was a lonely place to be. When I got older I acted as if I had left all the pain in the past. I didn't want people to look at me and see a victim. I was afraid that if I showed people who I really was they might not like me. They might not want to spend time with me. They might think I was damaged. I was so afraid of letting people see who I really was: someone who was carrying a lot of pain inside and someone who wasn't as strong as she pretended to be. I worried about what other people would think of me more than what I thought of myself. I wanted to be loved and liked. I took it personally when friends walked away, beating myself up inside about what I had possibly said or done to make them not want to spend time with me anymore. In the end I realised it was about them not me and that certain people had to leave my life so that I could embark on the healing journey that was needed. It may not have happened otherwise. I now know that being me means being vulnerable, letting people see all sides of me and hoping and trusting that they won't judge me and, if they do, I know it has nothing to do with me. I now have friends who accept me fully and it's much easier than trying to maintain the illusion I used to. I used try so hard to be a 'good' friend. Going above and beyond the call of duty because I felt I wasn't already enough. Friends left anyway. Now I know that some people are in our lives for a short time only. They teach us what we need to learn and then they are gone.

My journey gave me an understanding of my kids that I sometimes wonder would I have without my past. Instead of rejecting my experiences, I now embrace them. I thank them for what they taught me, because the love that has come into my life as a result of them is immeasurable.

Building that wall had protected me from hurt but it had also interfered with me experiencing any emotions completely. I was afraid to experience love fully too, and taking down the wall and being me, in all my glory, has allowed me to experience love like I didn't think existed.

I learned that who I am is ok. I am perfect as I am and I need and choose to be myself. It is ok to ask for what I need. If the only way I receive love is by neglecting myself and what I need, I will not be happy. I need to be me. It doesn't do us any good if the only way we receive love is by behaving a certain way or doing certain things to keep others happy. We need to be ourselves.

And with that knowledge, we knew that the kids needed to be themselves too. They needed to be loved and accepted for who they are. Their feelings were real and deserved to be respected. And so we did our best to see the world from their point of view. They got upset about things that we wouldn't be upset about, they were afraid of things that we weren't afraid of, and of course their sense of humour was different to ours. However, when we looked at the world from where they saw it, we were able to understand them much better.

Sometimes at night one of them would let their imagination run away with them (probably because of all the mad games they had played earlier) and they would be lying in bed afraid of monsters in the wardrobe or under the bed. At the start I did the normal thing which was to sit on the bed and explain that there were no such things as monsters and that they were perfectly safe and I was just downstairs if they needed me. But that didn't really help. So I imagined what it must be like to be them, lying in bed and thinking there was something in the wardrobe that was going to jump out. One night when Laura started crying about something under the bed, I went up with a broom and I stood in the middle of the room and said "right, any monsters in the wardrobe or under the bed you better watch out because I'm coming to get you". I rattled the broom under the bed and in the wardrobe and 'caught' the monsters, opened the window, flung them out and called out after them "and don't come back or you'll have me to deal with". Well the look on Laura's face was priceless. The monsters were really and truly gone. She saw me throw them out. She 'knew' that the monsters had been there and, because she trusted me so much, she knew that they were gone.   After all, in her eyes, I was magic! The difference was looking at the world through her eyes.

It really helped me understand what was going on for them when I made the effort to see the world from their point of view. When I understood them I was able to help them. For example, when David was very small, about 12 months old, he just would not settle at bed time. He screamed and screamed each night and we went up and down to him, trying to soothe and settle him. I remember one day wondering what is going on with this fella that he is screaming instead of going to bed and to sleep like other babies. One day I climbed into his cot to try and understand what was going on inside his little head. I lay there looking out through the bars and imagined what it was like for him watching us walking out the door and realised that he must be scared not knowing if we would come back or not. I got a real sense of what was going through his mind. He had been with somebody all day and now suddenly he was alone. He didn't like it and was probably afraid that no one was going to come to him.

However, he still needed to go to bed and settle on his own so this is what we did. On the first night I sat inside the door opposite his cot where he could see me. He kept shouting: "out, out, out!" and, at the same time, reaching out with his arms to me. I just sat there. If he got very loud I said "I'm here David, I'm here". And as I sat there, he eventually settled down and went to sleep. The next night I moved on to the door jam and, when he kept crying, I just said: "I'm here, I'm here". Again he eventually went to sleep. The next night I moved outside the door and the same thing happened. I eventually made my way across the landing and down the stairs.

He couldn't see me at this point but he could hear me. He got to know that I was there if he needed me and that just because he couldn't see me it didn't mean I was gone. I could hear him and if he needed me I was there. We had the baby monitor on downstairs so I could hear him and, when he did call, I went to the stairs and called up: "I'm here" and he was happy. He needed reassurance and that was the realisation I got when I made the effort to see the world from his point of view. We had 15 steps on the stairs so it took about 3 weeks but he was then able to go to bed and to sleep on his own, knowing one of us was nearby.

We taught the kids to be proud of who they are and to be the best version of themselves that they could possibly be. We encouraged them to dig deep to find the strength we knew they had when things got difficult. When they had a decision to make, we asked them questions to help them find the answers for themselves.

I remember when I was a teenager my parents wanted me to get a job in a Bank or a Local Authority. This was where the secure jobs were and I would be "set up for life". I wanted to be a *Ban Garda* but was an inch too short to be accepted. That was it: I trained for and got a permanent and pensionable job in a Local Authority. It was as if someone had put me in a box and I didn't know I could get out. I stayed in that job for twenty years, becoming unhappier each year until eventually I got sick and had to leave.

These experiences taught me so much. I knew that I would let my children follow their dreams, however mad they might seem, because I knew that would make them happy. If they wanted something badly enough they would find a way and we would help them.

We watched them grow and knew what really interested them. We noticed when they seemed lost in another world, happy and content, doing something that they enjoyed. We wondered about the career they might choose and we often chatted and got them to dream about it and imagine it.

Our job was not to create what our children would become but nurture and support them in becoming the true version of themselves, whatever that may be.

We knew, from experience, that fear can get in the way of us doing what we really want to do, and we wanted the kids to understand this and be able to recognise when it was fear that was stopping them from stepping up to challenges they were facing on the way to living the kind of life they wanted.

Laura has always loved animals. She never had dolls but had lots of stuffed dogs and bears. She had a nurse's uniform, a little medicine bag and she loved taking care of her pet animals. She regularly brought home stray dogs and so we began to think that a career with animals would suit her, but in her final year at school she started talking about going to college to take a Business Course. We would have been happy with whatever she chose, if we knew it was what she really wanted.

One day I was walking with her (as I said earlier, this is a great way to have a difficult conversation as you are not looking directly at each other so there is no pressure) and we started chatting about what she was going to do after school. I asked her if she could imagine her ideal life in a few years' time. What would she be doing? "Oh" she said, "if I could wave a magic wand I would be working with animals, as a vet or veterinary nurse". So I asked her why she had been considering doing a business course in college. "I hate science" was her reply. We discussed this a bit more and we discovered that she was really afraid of doing science subjects in college as she was finding them difficult in school. The more we talked, the more she discovered that it was really fear that was holding her back from doing what she really wanted to do and becoming the true version of herself. I started to describe the science subjects as frogs and asked her: "if someone told you that, if you ate some live frogs every day for the next few years, you could have this job you really love, would you eat them?" Her reply was: "hell ya". She made a decision that she could "put up with" a few years of doing subjects she wasn't too keen on (eating frogs) in order to get what she really wanted. She focused on her science subjects in school for the rest of that year and often came out of evening study saying she didn't want any dinner because "I've eaten so many frogs". She has now qualified as a Veterinary Nurse.

Sometimes the kids need a little help to overcome fear and become their true selves.

Helping kids discover and be able to express who they really are is a great gift to give them. How many of us have waited years before we have the confidence to show the world who we really are? We are taught that it's not ok to be yourself. People might not like you and the most important thing is that people like you – right? No, the most important thing is that you like yourself.

When David told us he was gay, I'll be honest and say that, even though we had suspected he was, it was a shock when he finally said it. I cried for two whole days as I worried for him and this more difficult road I envisaged ahead of him. And then the pride came to the fore. I was so proud of this lad who was able to stand up and say: "this is who I am and I'm happy". Isn't this what we want for our kids? For them to be happy? We raised him to be proud of who he is and to be ok with who he is. To this day I'm immensely proud of him as I watch him move forward with his life, enjoying his job as an Industrial Chemist, indulging his love of music and languages, his many friends and being comfortable in his own skin. Who are we to say how someone should lead their life? This was proof for me that our role as parents - guiding and nurturing this lad to be the best human being he could possibly be - had been done. It would be up to himself from here on in. The journey wasn't always easy but it was worth it.

The kids have amazing strengths and gifts. We didn't want them to do anything just to keep us happy. We knew that they had to be happy with the choices they made and that all they had to do was take the first step towards what they wanted to do. We could empower them to make that choice and then step back a little, always in the background if they needed us. Once they were happy with that first step, they would be able to make decisions for themselves. We wanted them to find out for themselves what their role and purpose was going to be. They are individuals and on loan to us for a while. We were there to help them learn what really inspires them and makes them happy.

The process began very early on, and we are seeing the effect of it now. I feel really happy when I see the two of them, content with who they are and the lives they are creating for themselves.

What I learned:

We all need to be loved and accepted for who we are. The effort of trying to be something we are not eventually takes its toll on our health and sense of wellbeing.

I found life was a lot easier when I let go of the mask I wore to hide the pain from my childhood. I am now open about what happened to me. I know it wasn't my fault. I find it easier now to show that vulnerable side of me. I am human. I can be hurt. I have been hurt. It's who I am and it has contributed to me being the woman I am today.

I am ok. My scars have made me an incredible mum full of love. I now embrace all parts of myself. I'm proud of who I am and of what I have come through.

I learned that my kids need to be accepted for who they are too. They need to be themselves. They need to embrace all aspects of themselves and we, as parents, have a big role to play in helping them get there. By loving them and accepting them exactly as they are, they learn to know they are ok, they are enough. They need to be able to speak what is on their mind and for us to be ok with that. If they are angry they need to know it's ok to feel angry and that we will listen to them and really hear what is going on for them.

It is a huge gift to give our children, to accept them exactly as they are, with their weaknesses and strengths, their quirks, their sense of humour, their interests, their taste in clothes and food, their sexuality, their religious beliefs, their choice in boyfriends and girlfriends, their hobbies and career choices. It's all ok. They will find the road that is right for them, making mistakes along the way, if we are there supporting them, helping them up when they fall, encouraging them to keep going, to being the best version of themselves that they can be.

Chapter 13

"You've got to do your own growing no matter how tall your Grandfather was"

Wow, my life has been like a roller coaster ride. The greatest high was when I began to understand just how powerful I am. I can take control of my thoughts whenever I notice I am not feeling good. I understand that my thoughts create my feelings and so when I am not feeling good, I check in to see what exactly is going on in my head. I notice that I am either worrying about something in the future or fretting about something in the past. I understand that my thoughts get more negative as I get more stressed. I check in regularly to see what my emotions are telling me. I know that my happiness depends on me doing things that make me feel good and increasing the flow of energy inside me. I have a list of things I do that I know will instantly lift my energy. Salsa dancing, walking in the woods or by the beach, and listening to some uplifting music, are just some of the things I do that make me feel better. I am committed to being happy and I take responsibility for it. I don't expect anyone else to make me happy. I, and I alone am responsible for how I feel. That's not to say that I don't slip back every now and then and expect people to behave differently than they are, and I can still get upset if people behave in a way that I don't like, but in the end I know it comes back to me and how I am interpreting what is happening. I know that I react differently when my energy is low and so I change that first.

When I hand over the remote control to my feelings to someone else, I lose all power over how I feel, and I'm letting someone else push my buttons. I don't like that and I don't want someone else determining how I'm going to feel on any given day. I want to choose. I want to decide what kind of day I am going to have. I no longer let other people control how I feel.

I also have a couple of practices that I do every day to keep myself balanced and happy:

I meditate every day for about 15 minutes. This quietens my mind and helps me let go of any unpleasant emotions I might be feeling. I haven't mastered long meditations and I find 15 minutes suits me perfectly and I can always find the time for it.

I tune in regularly to see how I am feeling, and if I need to do something to make myself feel better I will do it.

I take a few minutes every day to just breathe deeply. This helps to bring me back into the moment if I find my mind starting to wander off into the future or back into the past again. It brings relaxation into my body and allows me to let go of any stress.

Every day I write down ten things in my life that I am grateful for. This helps me focus on all the good things I have in my life. So often we are busy striving for more in different areas of our lives that we forget about all the lovely things we already have.

Discovering *Reiki* and *EFT* has brought even more peace and happiness into my life and I give myself treatments regularly.

As the kids got older, I looked back on the positive changes I had made in my life, the struggles I had overcome and the difference it had made in my life.

I could have kept looking back and been upset about what had happened me, but I wanted something different badly enough to take responsibility for my own happiness. The past is gone and no matter how much I analyse it, think about it and get upset about it, nothing about it will change.

Once I learned all this and experienced the positive benefits of this new way of thinking, I wanted the kids to know that they could do this too.

We believed in them. We knew they were meant to be happy and that they had the power inside themselves to create a life that was exactly how they wanted it to be. From our own experiences we had some really good tools we could pass on to them to help them on their journey. It was important that they knew how to be happy, learned to trust themselves, and their choices, and be able to create the kind of life they wanted.

Emotional maturity is often neglected in school with the emphasis being on academic subjects and how well you perform. However, being able to be a good friend, understanding what makes you feel good, and what doesn't, and being able to say no, are just as important. It was important that they learned that they are responsible for their own emotions no matter what anyone in their lives does. Teaching them that they have a choice in how they respond to situations and people in their lives was a fantastic lesson that we were able to give them. We all still struggle with this at times but in the end we know that it comes back to a choice that *we* can make: to be happy or not.

When my brother and I were young, there was usually a day, near the end of the summer, when we would be swimming in the sea. I can remember the two of us floating in the water and enjoying the warmth of the sun and feel of the water. We'd start talking about a day when the cold, wet weather would set in and we would be sitting in the car in the dark on the way to school. We knew we could bring back those feelings we had on that lovely summer day any time we needed to feel good - simply by thinking about that lovely day again. Unknown to myself, I was discovering that my thoughts really did determine how I felt. I taught this lesson to the kids and they used it often when they were having a particularly nice time. They would take in everything around them, the sights, the sounds, the tastes and the feelings, and on a bad day they were able to recreate all those lovely feelings again. They were learning how to take charge of their feelings.

Remembering my dreams of being a mum, and having a happy home, and the pictures I used create in my head of what it would be like, and then seeing how it came true, gave me something else to teach the kids. From a young age we used get them to imagine things. Imagine if you could fly. Imagine if you were a dog. Imagine if you were inside the story book. They used chat about what it would be like and they could "see" what it would be like in their heads.

When they were older we used get them to imagine their dream job. What would they be doing? When they got bogged down in study around Leaving Certificate time, we used get them to create a picture in their heads of the day they would get the results. How would they feel? What would they say? We used chat about it over and over again, imagining how thrilled they would be when they got the points they needed to do the course they wanted to do. We were driving home from the school the day Laura got her results and she turned to me and said: "Do you remember when we used talk about this day and what it would be like? This is exactly how I imagined it".

We trusted them. When they got an idea we encouraged them to run with it and see how it would turn out.

One summer when they were approximately 9 and 11 years old, they decided they wanted to earn extra money. They came up with a plan to paint round stones black and red to look like ladybirds. These would make lovely ornaments for people's gardens. We bought them the first two cans of paint and paintbrushes and they got to work in the garden shed. When their garden ornaments were ready, they set up a little stall outside the front gate. They stood there day after day selling these beautiful stones to people passing by with one of us keeping a watchful eye from inside the window. They sold all the stones and got to work on another batch. Eventually they tired of it and moved on to something else. I remember a neighbour saying to me how she would never allow her kids do something like that because she considered it begging. We all look at things differently and we really felt that the kids would learn a lot from the experience. They created something themselves and they sold it for a profit. We were very proud of their creativity and they were immensely proud of themselves. I use one of those stones today as a paperweight and it is a constant reminder to me of growth, change and courage.

At another time they took on a paper round. In good weather and bad, they had to go from house to house delivering papers. They couldn't decide one week not to deliver them as people were depending on them. They learned about responsibility and it instilled in them a desire to work hard in school so that they could create a good life for themselves. Paper rounds were a difficult way to earn money…

We all need to grow. We get stagnant if we stand still and so we keep getting that urge to do or learn something new. Sometimes it's something difficult we want to do and it can leave us feeling paralysed with fear. What is happening is we are looking to step out of where we feel comfortable and that feels scary. Teaching David and Laura to push the boundaries and step out of their comfort zone was a skill they learnt by our example. John and I have constantly stretched ourselves over the years, changing jobs, careers, and challenging ourselves with new ways of thinking. They heard us talking about our fears and our challenges and they rejoiced with us when we made the leap and felt the satisfaction of doing so.

Teaching David and Laura how to do this, I hope, will ensure they will always be able to stretch the boundaries of what makes them feel safe so that they can continue to grow too. It can seem very daunting to do something new and so we taught them to take baby steps and to clarify what it is they want to achieve. Rather than them feeling that they were jumping out into the unknown, we taught them to contain it and clarify exactly what this next step they wanted to take was. We showed them that they have already moved out of their comfort zones on lots of occasions i.e. starting at a new school, going to Irish College, going away from home for a weekend, making new friends etc. These have all been examples of them stretching themselves, so they knew they could do it. Each time they did, it then became easier and easier. Of course as they get older, the challenges they face and the steps out of their comfort zone, get bigger and bigger. David has left all his friends here and moved away to another town to work in a very challenging environment, and Laura has lived in Slovakia for a number of months and is now travelling over and back to work in Kuwait. If I had told them ten years ago they would be doing this, I don't think they would have believed me.

We allowed them make mistakes and taught them that it's ok, because that's how we learn. They now know that when they make a mistake or something happens that they are not happy about, it is either an opportunity for them to learn, or simply meant to be, and so they look at these experiences in a different way. Our motto for a long time back has been: "Everything is happening perfectly". When something goes 'wrong', they analyse it to see why and what it is they need to learn from it or why it actually, in the long run, may be the best thing that has happened. What I notice is that, after the initial frustration with what has happened, they quickly switch to looking at the situation differently and they continue to feel good rather than feeling down about it.

The bigger picture here was teaching and helping them discover new ideas, new ways of thinking and behaving.

Now they both trust that the events that happen in their lives are there for a reason and are open to whatever curve balls life throws at them.

Chapter 14

"To forgive is to set a prisoner free and discover that the prisoner was you"
- Lewis B Smedes

I loved those years with the kids, the feeling of knowing that if I simply loved them and accepted them for who they are I would not go too far wrong. And so I loved them and then loved them some more. I did my best to put myself in their shoes and try to see what they might need and did my best to give it to them. It was simple really. I felt happy and safe playing an important role in their lives. We had lots of fun and I felt loved. I thought that was it. I had arrived. I sailed along feeling happy and content in most areas of my life. My home life was great but work was not. I had studied and worked hard to receive promotions and with each step up the ladder I had become more and more unhappy. The work I was doing was not fulfilling me in any way. I was dragging myself into work knowing in my heart that I should be doing something else. I knew that if I died in the morning I would simply be replaced. I was a number and that was all. However I was in a permanent pensionable job and people didn't give that up too easily. One day, while out walking, I noticed a pain in my hip that had not been there before. Each day I went walking the pain became worse and worse. Then I began to get the pain while I was sitting at work. Then I began to have it for a lot of the day. And then I had it all the time. Over a period of a few months I went from being a healthy woman who loved to walk three or four miles almost every day to one who could no longer walk as far as the gate to collect the post. I eventually needed crutches to get about as the pain was so bad. I had to take lots of pain killers and my life suddenly got turned upside down. I had to leave my job because I could no longer sit at my desk. I couldn't understand what was happening to me and I became very unhappy believing that life as

I knew it was over. Despite visits to physiotherapists, rheumatologists, chiropractors, orthopaedic surgeons etc. no one could find what the problem actually was and yet I was crippled in pain.

I began to read books about illness, where it can come from, the part that our emotions play in our health and I was hooked. I was fascinated from the start and began to read everything I could get my hands on relating to the subject.

I began to wonder about myself and what this pain was about. I knew from the books I had read that there was more to it than just the physical pain. I wondered if, despite the fact that I had healed so much of the emotional pain from my past, there was still stuff there that had not been dealt with fully. I knew that if I thought back to my early years and dwelt on the memories I could still get upset and this, according to the books I had read, indicated that there was still more healing needed.

I went for a session with a person trained in a therapy that was to change my life as it was a process that quickly eliminated negative emotions from the past. The process meant that I was still able to remember my past but the emotions that I felt when I thought about them were no longer accessible. This was to change the rest of my life for the better. I became fascinated with the subject of our emotions and the part they play in our health. I began to study different therapies, completely fascinated by the idea of us healing ourselves. I received treatments that brought my body back into a state of balance which allowed my own natural healing system to kick in and do what it was designed to do: heal me. The pain started to ease and I began to walk again. Soon I was back walking four miles a day and enjoying every minute of it. I realised that being unhappy in my work had taken a huge toll on my health. It had caused severe stress that had eventually manifested itself physically. I wanted to learn more and so I went on to train in several therapies including *Reiki* and *EFT* and am now a Trainer teaching these therapies to others so that they can take responsibility for their own healing. I felt empowered and back on track because I had acknowledged that another need I had was to grow. I couldn't stay the same and be happy. I needed to learn more and more. I needed to evolve and become the best version of me that I could. And that's what I did. I read many books with similar themes and I began to understand my journey. I started to see clients, working with them, helping them to find peace and happiness in their lives again.

The training reiterated what I already knew; that I and I alone am responsible for my feelings. I can choose to let people upset me or I can choose to be happy. Day by day I make the choice to be happy. That was the biggest lesson I learned. I always have a choice.

One day, about eight years ago in early December, I was driving home alone from a course. I was feeling really good thinking back over the week, the people I had met, the fun we had and all the things I had learned. Then the hymn "Oh Holy Night" came on the radio. As I drove along listening to this beautiful song, a feeling came over me that I had never felt before. It was a feeling of pure bliss, pure happiness and absolute love. I had to stop the car as the feeling was so intense. From the depths of my soul I shouted out in the car: "I forgive you", "I forgive you", "I forgive you" and, for the first time, I really meant it. I felt the last of the pain and regret for my past leave my body and I was finally, totally and completely free.

What an amazing journey this is that I am on.

When I look back at the person I was thirty years ago I hardly recognise her. I look at photos and can remember the pain that I was keeping deep inside. I can see it in my eyes: the shame, the fear, the sadness, the anger and the hurt.

I was a woman who wanted to leave the pain behind and move on with my life. I see the wall I built around me to protect myself from more pain. I see the determination to create something different. I asked for something different: a happy family and kids to love. I dreamed about it as a child and acted as if I had it already with my dolls. I could see it in my mind. I knew I would have it. I didn't know how but I really believed I would and so I took the first step. I pretended I was the mum I wanted to be. I acted as if I already was the person I wanted to be. I opened my heart, the heart that felt battered and bruised. I was willing to try again, to trust again. I loved and I was loved back. I loved some more and I received even more. My heart is overflowing with love for my family and they love me. My heart has mended.

The most amazing part of this, and something that some people cannot understand, is that I have forgiven my Dad. This was a gift to myself. It's not about him. I'm not saying that what happened was ok but I am willing to no longer let it have any hold over me. What I do have is a deep sense of compassion for him as I believe he must have been badly hurt as a child too. I feel sad for him when I think of the conflict that must have been inside him: so religious, so fearful of God and yet doing these things. He was not as lucky as I am. He carried his pain all his life. He never reached the place that I did and I'm sorry about that. I wish, for his sake, that he had. As I look back on the journey I have been on, I am deeply grateful for the childhood experiences that led me here. I may never have learnt to love as much as I have loved without them and I may never have been loved as much in return.

I was asked recently by Laura what else I wanted to do with my life. Pausing for a moment to think, I found myself replying: "I have everything I ever wanted".

CHAPTER 15

"FROM WHAT WE GET, WE CAN MAKE A LIVING; WHAT WE GIVE, HOWEVER, MAKES A LIFE" - ARTHUR ASHE

I know that my life has meaning, that there is a reason I am here. Over the years, I often asked myself: "Who am I?" and "Why am I here?" I began my journey wondering why I had the experiences I had, pretending they didn't matter and attempting to put them in the past, but now I know and accept that they are part of my journey. I would not be where I am today without them and, crazy as this sounds, I am grateful for them, because I have discovered why I am here. My purpose is to make a difference and help others, some of whom have had similar experiences, see that there is life afterwards and not just an ordinary life but a wonderful life full of love and happiness if you want to have it. My growth has come from accepting this part of myself as a very important part. It is a part of my past and it has contributed to shaping me and moulding me into the woman I am. I learnt so much over the years that I may possibly not have learnt without my experiences. I may never have reached the low that literally propelled me into finding all the good stuff in life. I may have drifted along never feeling any intensity of emotions.

I have learnt that our very essence is love. We are made of energy and that energy is love. When we are afraid of what people will think or what will happen, when we feel shame, anger or hurt, we have simply moved away from love. Feeling love is where we need to be in order to find happiness. Living in each moment, instead of thinking back to the past or worrying about the future, is the secret I found to happiness. I trust and believe that everything happens for a reason.

I absolutely love the work I now do: helping men and women on a daily basis move forward from all sorts of pain, including childhood abuse or neglect, bereavements, accidents, separation and so on, as well as those suffering from physical ailments. I love working with youngsters who are finding life difficult because they don't feel they 'fit in'. I can help them see how perfect they are just as they are and show them how to find their own strengths instead of trying to fit in with the crowd. This is so rewarding. Their parents learn too how to love their child just as they are and accept them as the unique people they are.

Research has shown that the good feelings you experience when helping others can be just as important to your health as exercise and a healthy diet. That feeling you get when you realise you are really making a difference in someone's life is one of the greatest feelings in the world.

And so our children need to give in order to be happy. Did you ever sit with a child and offer them a toy only for them to hand it back to you? Very young children will pick a flower and offer it to you. They want to help and want to give. Giving them the opportunity to give is an important step in their development. They will not be happy if all they do is take. They feel good when they give and they learn from watching us. When we show compassion to others our children learn to be compassionate.

When I was growing up I never saw someone in need turned away from the door without them receiving something and it was something we continued in our home. My Dad, despite his faults, was a very religious man and a very generous one. He always ensured he had someone who was less well off than himself to take care of. He would bring a dinner to someone in need nearly every night and regularly gave money to charity. He involved us in this too and we were always aware that there were people who didn't have what we had. This stayed with me and one day a lady who used call to me regularly and who had a lot of children, came and asked for help to buy one of her children a bicycle as he had grown out of the one he had. I was going to give her some money to help but David and Laura, who had been listening in the hallway, suddenly ran out to the back garden. They brought out a bicycle and wheeled it out the door to the lady for her little boy. I was speechless and quite taken aback at this show of compassion from my two kids for another who had so little. When I asked them about it they said they had lots of things to play with and they would ask Santa for another one! What could I say? There is a need in all of us to give to others and we feel wonderful when we find a way to give something that means a lot to someone else.

Allowing our kids to give and finding opportunities for them to do so, accepting what they offer with grace, can help them grow up fulfilling their purpose in this amazing world. Being enthusiastic in our role and being present with our kids teaches them to be the same in whatever role they choose. Our job as parents is done, they love us but they certainly don't need us as much as they did and that's a sign of a job well done. We have looked on with pride when we see one buying a bag of dog food for animal shelters, jumping out of planes to raise money for unfortunate animals and the other being a good friend to those who need him, helping friends study and volunteering in the scouts, enabling younger kids have the experiences he did when he was young.

They know that helping and giving to others makes them feel good.

Chapter 16

"Don't cry because it's over – smile because it happened", Dr. Seuss

The kids are grown up and have left home.

Sometimes I'm sad because those days with them when they were small are over. They no longer want me to read to them or play dress up. I no longer hear their giggles or their fighting and their stuff is no longer around the house. No more wet towels on the floor in the bathroom and no more driving them to music or basketball.

The days of holding them in my arms and dancing around the kitchen floor are over and there are no more paintings being brought home to stick on the fridge.

The house is quiet and has returned to the way it was in the beginning: John, myself and the dog.

I have fantastic memories and I smile when I look back at the photos from when they were little. It went by so fast in the end even though sometimes it seemed like they would never grow up.

Now my son is taller than I am and reaches out to me to give me a hug. My daughter still loves a hug and is not a bit shy in letting me know when she wants one. They both give me so much love that my heart is overflowing. They never stop showing us how much they love us and I know they appreciate the effort we made.

They are lovely, kind and caring young adults with hearts full of love for themselves and others, ready to go out into the world and share that love with others. What more could I have wished for? I have no regrets and I'm glad of that. I found the magic. I found a real strength and determination inside me. I took the chance, became vulnerable and opened my heart to love again. The rewards have been huge.

David and Laura taught me so much and I will be forever thankful to them

I treasure a couple of things in particular that they have said recently.

Laura:

"Mum, I'm so proud of you. You need to write this book so that when I have kids of my own I can raise them exactly as you and Dad raised us".

David:

"It's only now that I am older I realise just how much you and Dad did for us. Not in what you bought us or places you brought us to, but actually how much you loved us".

A heart filled with love has no choice but to heal….

You have magic kisses too……

CHAPTER 17

THE JOURNEY CONTINUES

"Happiness is a journey not a destination.
Work like you don't need money, love as if you've never been hurt
and dance like no one is looking."

Healing and awareness continue for me. The children have grown up and the journey goes on. They were the beginning of my healing and it continues each day. When I wake up I have choices to make. I choose to be happy and I choose to love. I choose to be grateful for all my experiences and all that I have in my life. I choose to meditate to still my mind and connect with myself. I am aware of the thoughts in my head and if they make me feel good, I allow them to continue and, if not, I choose to change them. I choose how I respond to situations in my life and I rejoice in the fact that I know I can.

I look at situations where someone wants to have an argument with me as an 'invitation to dance' and I usually choose to 'sit this one out'. People sometimes seek out arguments so that they can vent anger and sadness they feel inside. Sometimes they know of no other way to make the pain inside them go away. Recognising their pain, instead of taking it personally and thinking I'm being attacked, helps me to stay out of situations that can end up making me feel bad. I can then wait for an opportunity to help the person voice what is really going on with them when they are feeling calmer.

I take responsibility for my happiness and no longer blame others for how I feel. I regularly spend time alone recharging my batteries by walking, dancing, reading inspiring books and listening to uplifting music. I take each day as it comes and do my best to live in that day only. I try to live by the *Reiki* principles as they help to keep me focused on the here and now. If I live in the past I can be filled with sadness and regret, and if I live in the future I can be worried and frightened. When I live in the present moment I have enough of everything, love, shelter, money, peace, happiness etc.

Just for today I am free from anger.

Just for today I am free from worry.

Just for today I will count my many blessings.

Just for today I will do my work honestly.

Just for today I will be kind to every living creature.

Life goes on and difficult people and situations keep coming my way. But now I know the secret. The secret is love. When I get angry everything seems to go wrong and fall apart. When I stop for a moment and make the choice to feel compassion for others, when I step in to their shoes for a minute and try to see the world through their eyes, I can see and understand the pain they are in and why they are behaving as they are. I recognise them as just other human beings feeling hurt and pain and trying to make themselves feel better. It's not always easy and sometimes I choose to walk away from people in my life for a while if it becomes too difficult. Some people inflict so much pain that I find my journey is to love myself enough to walk away. This can bring criticism but I am confident enough now to know what is right and wrong for myself, and I'm not afraid to act on it, even if others think I should behave differently. I care for myself and treat myself as my best friend. I am kind to myself and do things that make me happy.

Sometimes I slip back into feeling fear, anger, sadness and hurt and then I can feel my life start to go askew. Everything becomes difficult. John and I had a very difficult experience recently where we both felt intense anger and resentment towards someone who had done something very wrong towards us. We both got caught up in very negative feelings and both felt completely stressed and overwhelmed. Nothing was going right for us in how we were dealing with the situation. One day the penny dropped for me and I realised I had wandered away from the path I knew I needed to be on. I sat for a while and began to see why the other person might have been behaving in this way. I began to see the world through her eyes and realised the pain she could be feeling. This brought me to feeling compassion for her and the anger and resentment fell away. Straight away the situation began to turn around for the better with everything we needed to sort out the situation coming to hand. Maintaining that feeling of compassion for her throughout made the journey easier. There were still days when I felt angry and resentful but I knew where I needed to be if I wanted a good solution for all concerned. Each time I felt the negative feelings arise, I stopped and moved to feeling compassion again. The situation ended with the truth becoming clear.

I have learnt that no matter what life brings to my door I know I will be able to handle it. I'll cope by choosing to feel love instead of negative feelings. I know that every experience I have is one for me to learn that feeling love and compassion is the answer. Love and compassion for myself and others.

My family is still very important to me and we regularly spend time together. I still love to play and I notice that my 'kids' still do too, as I discovered recently when I found three tennis rackets and a ball and the three of us played 'tennis' up and down the road laughing and joking with each other and generally enjoying the fun.

Life is short and we are meant to be happy. I believe every experience is an opportunity to learn something. In the past I would think there was something new to be learned in each of our experiences but recently I've discovered that for me it's the same lesson each time.

Our natural state is one of love and our journey is to remember that over and over again.

x

"You are doing a fabulous job, no matter how hard the journey may be remember to be kind to yourself, you are doing the best you can.

You are amazing and beautiful – Every Day.

Don't ever tell yourself anything less", Erin Bella Bleu.

AFTERWARD

THE KIDS HAVE THEIR SAY

DAVID

Just like the Aaron Neville song – "*The Voyage*' - Mum and Dad were the captains of the ship and Laura and I were the crew, together with Sandy the dog of course. We were Team Collins. No matter what happened us during any particular day at school or at after school activities, we always came home to the Team Collins bubble - it was the four of us in it together... always.

As a kid, at school, I was teased quite a bit over things like the colour of my hair and the fact that I preferred music to sport. I tried hard to like sport but I always went back to listening to music or playing the piano. My parents introduced me to lots of activities so that I could find something I enjoyed doing. They seemed to want me to have fun. I tried soccer, hurling, swimming, scouts, drama, French classes and piano lessons... My parents allowed me to choose myself and never forced me to do any activity I didn't like.

Eventually I figured out I enjoyed music and scouts and after a few years I found myself as the keyboardist and backing singer of the newest band in town, gigging around Ireland and doing what I loved. I also became a Scout Leader, climbing the highest mountains and going survival camping just for fun!

My parents put up with the loud music and the smelly campfire clothes and loved that I was happy. I was good at something, making lots of friends, and I loved it.

My parents always taught me to be proud of who I am and not to let others bring me down. We were always talking and I could tell them anything. I remember when I was about fourteen years old Mum asked me to go for a walk with her. We chatted as usual and this time the topic that came up was about girls. My Mum told me that liking boys and girls and having mixed feelings was perfectly normal at this age. She told me that she and Dad love me and would always love me whether I ended up liking boys or girls. At the time I didn't realise the significance of this chat and didn't really take much notice but years later when I realised I was gay, I knew I could tell them without any hassle. When I broke the news to Mum and Dad they hugged me and said that as long as I was happy, they were happy. We talked about it and laughed about it and that made it feel extremely normal. They made me feel loved and the fact that we were able to joke about it made us all feel more comfortable.

Of course everything wasn't always hunky-dory. I threw a lot of tantrums as a kid and being the eldest I tended to test the boundaries quite frequently. But more often than not those arguments ended up with my Mum and me sitting down and discussing what had happened and each of us sharing how we felt. I gradually began to understand how my actions affected other people and that upsetting someone I love didn't make me feel good. There was always something to be learned from these situations - slowly... but surely.

Mum and Dad always wanted the world for Laura and me. They taught us valuable lessons that instilled a sense of pride, self-worth, ambition, a passion for fun and adventure and the feeling of being loved unconditionally. Recently, at the age of twenty four, during dinner (and after a few glasses of wine), I told my parents for the first time of how thankful I am to have such amazing parents as them. I told them that only now as an adult can I look back and really appreciate all they did for us, the sacrifices they made and the huge effort they put in to raising us, and how in years to come if I become half the parents they are - I know I'll be doing a good job.

LAURA

I can't remember everything in my childhood but the one theme that has been constant is love. There were no worries about family life – we were and still are Team Collins. Team Collins is a term that came about on a holiday when I was about fourteen years old and I think it's a great way to describe the four of us. I was quite a quirky kid. I was never into dresses, make up and dancing. I loved playing in the back garden, climbing the tree we had out there, playing basketball and hosing down the garden path in the winter to make a skate path when it iced over. Although many mums might want their daughter to like wearing dresses and putting on make-up etc., my Mum was happy if I was happy. Often that meant shopping in the boys' clothes section in shops. I look back on old photos and cringe a little at the boyish look I had but I wouldn't change it for anything. I remember being really happy and can now appreciate Mum and Dad for letting me dress and look the way I wanted. It allowed me to be really comfortable with who I was, love myself from a young age, and not worry too much about what others thought of me.

When I look back on my childhood I remember Coronation Street and bath times on Sunday night. I remember being tucked in each night with a goodnight kiss being planted on every single teddy I had in the bed with me (quite a few), and Mum saying a special goodnight to each one of them, remembering all their names! I remember all of the activities I took part in, from violin playing, to piano playing, horse riding, swimming clubs, basketball camps, scouts, and sleep overs. At one of these sleep overs Mum heard us all awake one morning at three am and she came down to make hot chocolate for all of us! She was the coolest Mum ever according to my friends after making that hot chocolate!! I always wondered why other kids my age were "so embarrassed" by their Mums and Dads. I looked at mine and couldn't think of two cooler people.

We did a lot of things as a family. Cycling and walking in the woods were the main ones. We were always chatting about our day, our friends, the different activities we did and what we were excited for.

I laugh when I look back on 6th class in primary school. I was eleven years old and my best friend was fighting with her Mum and wasn't speaking to her. I imagined what it would be like to not speak to my Mum…. to not tell her about my day when she picked me up from school. One day I decided to try it out. She picked me up from school and I tried not talking to her, saying the bare minimum and acting grumpy. It was the most difficult thing I had ever attempted and I gave in a few hours after school, bursting to tell her all the exciting news of what had happened in the few hours I was away from her. The funny thing was she allowed me to just be that way, accepting my mood and not pushing me to be any different. I couldn't keep it up though because I loved telling her everything and she listened so well.

As I said I was quite a quirky kid growing up. I was never going to be happy as a person who hid their true feelings and acted "cool". I was just me and people seemed to like who I was all the way through primary school. Secondary school arrived and I wasn't prepared for the difficulty of maintaining who I was. I felt like people wanted me to be a completely different person than the slightly crazy, energetic girl that I was. The image other girls portrayed was one of "too cool for school", whereas I was just so excited to be learning new things, to be with new people, to meet new teachers and to get to know this new school. I remember lying in bed crying one night, so confused as to why people didn't seem to like who I was. Mum crawled in beside me and asked what was wrong. After explaining my problem she took a while to answer, clearly not wanting to give the wrong advice at this significant and vulnerable moment in my life. She said the kids in my year had all grown up in different houses, in different schools, and they had all had different experiences. They might not be used to seeing someone like me who was so comfortable with who she was with no mask of coolness, just my "Laura-face". She advised me to tone down my craziness just a little bit but to maintain who I was as a person. She told me to hold on to my passion for reading, for teddies and basketball and whatever else I was passionate about. To never lose myself.

I've always been able to turn to Mum and Dad with problems I had no matter how trivial or how big they were. There was no way I could have a problem and try and deal with it by myself. I always let them know what was going on. I think that is what kept our relationship so strong. Communication meant that they always knew and understood why things upset me.

On the 5th of December 2013 I had a meeting with a guidance councillor in my college. I was wondering what add on course I should do from my veterinary nursing course to be able to apply for Veterinary Medicine in UCD. After a long chat and a phone call to a past student, I found out about Kosice: a city in Slovakia that had a Veterinary Medicine University that was quite easy to get accepted into after obtaining a science degree. My head spun. It had always been the plan that I would do an extra year in Athlone and then apply for the Veterinary Medicine programme. Suddenly everything was brought forward a year. Mum and Dad were on holidays so I couldn't call them to tell them about it. I didn't want to disturb the holiday by telling them about this new, very realistic opportunity that was just around the corner. I walked about 13km that day just thinking about it. My head was bursting and I couldn't believe my dream was so possible and close. Then the phone rang. I was out of breath and still walking, so when I answered I was surprised to hear Mum's voice. She knew straight away that I was worried about something and eventually dragged the news out of me. They have been totally supportive in helping me achieve what I want.

From funding my education, to almost daily Skype calls, they are always there for me when I need them.

When I found the course too stressful they guided and supported me as I made the difficult decision to leave the Veterinary Medicine Course and take a different path.

Looking back at the past twenty two years, I wouldn't change a thing. A few years ago I jokingly said to Mum that she should write a parenting book, outlining everything she and Dad had done with David and me, so that someday I could have it all to hand for raising my own kids. Little did I know that she had felt the need to write this book for a long time. She wanted to share her story to help other people: to show that the chain of abuse can be broken. Without her strength and determination for us to experience a really happy childhood, I wouldn't be the strong, confident and ambitious young woman I am today.

She didn't break the chain of abuse; Mum smashed that shackle and healed the wounds it left behind. Mum sees and lives life through love, and because of that, I believe I do as well.

About the Author

Ber Collins is a woman on a mission to ensure that kids grow up in happy homes filled with love and fun. Her unique experiences have given her an insight into the challenges being faced by Mums especially those who have had a difficult childhood. She works with clients who are committed to moving forward: guiding, motivating and inspiring them to be the Mum their kids need them to be.

She works from her clinic in Co. Clare in Ireland where she lives with her husband John and dog Fleur.

Release your Magic

I am passionate about helping Mums who are stressed and overwhelmed become the Mum that they want to be.

To avail of some free tips and advice come over and connect with me.

Website: www.bercollins.com

Facebook: www.facebook.com/everymumhasmagickisses

I would love to see you there.

Ber xx

#releaseyourmagic